Casebook in Abnormal Psychology

Casebook in Abnormal Psychology

John Vitkus
Barnard College

Random House New York

To my wife, Lisa

First Edition
98765432

ISBN: 0-394-37942-X

Cover photo: Joseph Mulligan
Cover design: Sandra Josephson
Text design: Stacey Alexander

Manufactured in the United States of America

INTRODUCTION

The *Casebook in Abnormal Psychology* consists of a selection of eleven different psychiatric case histories representing several major areas of abnormal psychology including, Anxiety Disorders, Mood Disorders, Psychotic Disorders, and Childhood Disorders. The diagnoses follow the conventions of the *Diagnostic and Statistical Manual of Mental Disorders, Third Edition-Revised* (American Psychiatric Association, 1987), commonly abbreviated as simply *DSM-III-R*. Any exceptions are noted at the end of each case.

Each case is presented with a particular treatment. The treatments represent basic approaches to abnormal psychology: Psychodynamic, Cognitive-Behavioral, Sociocultural, Neuroscience, and Eclectic. The *Casebook in Abnormal Psychology* is meant to be used as a supplement for any textbook in abnormal psychology such as *Abnormal Psychology: Current Perspectives*, Fifth Edition, by Richard R. Bootzin and Joan Ross Acocella. Consequently, the therapy descriptions presented are only general descriptions of the processes involved in psychotherapy. For a more detailed discussion of the theoretical foundations and therapeutic techniques of any particular approach to therapy, readers should refer to their texts, practitioners' guides, or therapy handbooks.

The cases in this book are based on actual material provided by practicing psychiatrists and psychologists. The presenting symptoms described in this casebook were actually observed, and the therapeutic techniques utilized in treatment were actually administered. However, because of the need to maintain confidentiality, details such as names, gender, occupations, and places that may identify particular individuals have been changed. In many cases, symptoms and treatments from different people have been combined into one case. Any resemblance to real persons is purely coincidental.

CASE ORGANIZATION

Each case is organized into five sections: Presenting Complaint, Personal History, Conceptualization and Treatment, Prognosis, and Discussion. These categories reflect, in a general way, how psychiatric professionals organize their cases and describe them.

The **presenting complaint** refers to the various symptoms and circumstances that prompted the person to seek psychiatric help. Most often this information is collected at the first therapy session, which usually involves an initial interview. In some instances, family members are relied upon as primary information sources because the individual is unable to provide an adequate account of his or her symptoms. An example of this might be a woman suffering from Alzheimer's disease or a child with Separation Anxiety Disorder.

The **personal history** section provides background information that the therapist may find helpful in diagnosing and treating the person. Unlike a person's presenting complaint, the person's personal history is actively solicited by the therapist. As a result, these histories vary greatly from case to case, depending on what the particular therapist may find useful. For example, traditional psychodynamic therapists often devote a great deal of time in therapy to obtaining a detailed account of the person's childhood in the hopes of uncovering the unconscious conflicts that may afflict the person. Since, according to this view, a person's symptoms are merely superficial manifestations of underlying unconscious traumas, knowing the precise nature of these symptoms is important only because it can provide clues to the latent problems. More important are the various clues that may shed light on the person's unconscious (e.g., dreams, fears, etc.) In contrast, most behavior therapists are concerned primarily with the objective history of the disorder: the form of the symptoms, when and under what circumstances the symptoms first appeared, and so forth. For these therapists, a knowledge of the person's dreams or childhood memories is irrelevant and therefore unimportant. A particularly interesting comparison can be found in the case histories of Generalized Anxiety Disorder and Dysthymic Disorder.

The differences between various theoretical approaches becomes most evident when one examines the way in which therapists formulate their treatment plans and implement them. The next section, **conceptualization and treatment,** focuses on these processes. The case conceptualization refers to how the therapist organizes the case and makes sense of the person's symptoms. The therapist draws together different information from the person's complaints and history and then pieces them together to form a coherent picture of the disorder. The therapist uses these facts to determine an official diagnosis. To help clarify these diagnoses, a definition of the relevant *DSM-III-R* disorder also appears in this section.

The treatment section documents the exact methods used to implement the treatment plan. Specific therapy techniques are described in as much detail as possible. In most of the cases, segments of actual dialogues between the therapist and the person seeking treatment are included. The aim of this section is to give the reader a concrete and vivid impression of what actually occurs in the therapy session.

Readers must keep in mind that the therapy approach presented with each case is not the only treatment available; virtually every disorder may be treated by a variety of different therapeutic programs. By presenting a particular treatment with each disorder, it is *not* intended to imply that the form of treatment presented is the most effective—or even the most common—treatment for that particular disorder. (However, in no case is a therapy inappropriate for its diagnosis.) Instead, the aim of providing specific treatments along with each case is to expose readers to the specific techniques commonly practiced by psychiatric professionals of different theoretical orientations. By describing specific therapeutic techniques, it is hoped that readers will gain a clearer concept of how different theoretical approaches are employed in the course of therapy.

The case **prognosis** refers to the therapist's prediction of how the person will function after therapy. In some cases, the person is expected to be more or less cured of his or her disorder. In other cases, the person is predicted to relapse. In the more chronic cases, the person is not expected to show a significant improvement in the foreseeable future and will in all likelihood continue to deteriorate. These prognoses are based on both the individual's response to therapy and on the typical response most people with this disorder show. Keep in mind, however, that therapists will tend to present cases that have been treated successfully, and consequently the prognoses for these case histories may be more optimistic than population norms would suggest.

Finally the **discussion** section describes any aspect of the case history that was atypical or otherwise noteworthy. This section mentions if a person was given any unusual treatment techniques or if therapy was performed in an unusual way. Other therapy techniques that are commonly used to treat the disorder are pointed out. This section also reviews the therapist's personal approach to the case. It discusses how the therapist's own conceptualization of the person's problem determined the information they sought in the person's history and the particular treatments they employed.

THE PURPOSES OF THIS CASEBOOK

There are three main purposes of this casebook. The first is to provide readers with a detailed and vivid account of the symptoms that characterize various disorders. For example, many descriptions of psychiatric disorders employ general terms such as describing an anxious man as being "para-lyzed by irrational fears." Although this description is accurate, it does not provide the same impression as noting that this man "worries about finding the 'perfect' suit to such an extent that he has not bought any clothes at all in over two years." Similarly, this casebook aims to provide a concrete view of how therapy is conducted. Using the same example, saying that the anxious man was "given a task-oriented homework assignment" is not as informative as providing actual dialogue in which the therapist gives the person direct instructions to go to a nearby clothing store. In short, the primary goal of this casebook is not to describe what different disorders and therapies are; it is to describe what these disorders and therapies are *like*.

It has been said that the psychotherapy a person receives is not determined so much by his or her symptoms as by the theoretical orientation of his or her therapist. The second purpose of this casebook is to highlight the differences in how various therapies are conducted. Many of these differenc-es are obvious. Some therapies last for weeks, others are life-long. Some focus on immediate concerns, some focus on past issues, and some attempt to treat both. In addition to these overt differences, various therapies contain more subtle discrepancies that may nevertheless affect a person's therapy in important ways. For example, some therapists refer to the people they treat as *clients*; others refer to them as *patients*. The difference between these two terms involves certain subtle yet clear implications for the person's role in the therapeutic process, specifically the client/patient's status *vis-a-vis* the thera-pist. As another example, some therapists insist that the person seeking therapy define the goals of treatment; other therapists maintain their own agenda. This distinction will have a great impact on the client/patient's status in therapy and, consequently, on the course of therapy and its duration. Many people are to some extent or another ignorant of the options available in therapy. By outlining the differences between various therapeu-tic approaches, it is hoped that this casebook will provide a clear picture of these options. Of course, this is of particular pragmatic value should the reader, or someone he or she knows, decide to seek psychiatric help.

Although this casebook discusses different treatment approaches as though they were clearly distinct, these differences tend in reality to be blurred. That is, practicing psychiatric professionals rarely ally themselves solely with one theoretical orientation; to varying degrees most therapists employ a more or less eclectic approach. This trend has been increasingly prevelant over the past decade. Evidence of this spreading eclecticism can be seen throughout this casebook—from psychodynamic therapists who em-ploy medications and situation manipulations to behavior therapists who interest themselves in the client/patient's subjective thoughts and feelings. Although an argument can be made for calling every form of therapy in this casebook "eclectic," for clarity's sake the cases presented here are labelled with the theoretical approach that forms the primary basis of each particular treatment.

The third purpose of this casebook is to illustrate the limitations of the psychiatric professional in everyday practice. For example, therapy that aims at achieving a dynamic insight is limited to those people who are intellectually capable of this accomplishment. Therapy for young or more seriously disturbed people would require some fundamental alterations. As another example, behavior therapists find themselves at a loss with people who conceptualize their problems in nonspecific terms. When the person says, "I want to be fulfilled" or "I want to be happier," the behavior therapist must first translate these rather vague goals into more concrete terms before therapy can proceed. Of course, all forms of psychotherapy will be limited in their ability to treat disorders involving psychosis or severe organic impairment. Most therapists would agree that pharmacotherapy (in some cases combined with supportive therapy for the person's family), is the only realistic approach for these disorders.

As a final note, it is hoped that this small, select sample of case studies will provide students with information on psychopathology and psychotherapy that is beyond the scope of their texts. More generally, it is hoped that readers will find this casebook stimulating and thought-provoking.

ACKNOWLEDGMENTS

First of all, I am very grateful to the following consultants for their time, help, and expertise. In addition to providing me with the basic information about the various diagnoses and the different forms of treatment, they gave me a fascinating behind-the-scenes view of therapy.

Ellie Bragar, Psy.D.
private practice, New York, NY

Howard A. Crystal, M.D.
Albert Einstein College of Medicine,
Yeshiva University, Bronx, NY

Zira DeFries, M.D.
Barnard College Health Service, New York, NY
private practice, New York, NY

John Fogelman, M.D.
St. Luke's/Roosevelt Hospital Center, New York, NY
private practice, Pomona, NY

Harriet N. Mischel, Ph.D.
private practice, New York, NY

Pat Pantone, Ph.D.
St. Luke's/Roosevelt Hospital Center, New York, NY
private practice, New York, NY

David Spiegel, M.D.
Stanford University Medical Center
Stanford University, Stanford, CA

B. Timothy Walsh, M.D.
Columbia/Presbyterian Medical Center, New York, NY

Special mention must be given to Richard Bootzin for his expert advice and guidance from the inception of this book to its completion.

I appreciate the insightful comments of Ronald Doctor, California State University at Northridge, for taking valuable time out of his busy schedule to review an early draft of this book. At Random House, I also wish to thank my editor, Rochelle Diogenes, who took some raw ideas and translated them into a workable project and Bob Greiner who shepherded this project through the publishing process. I am also indebted to Chrysoula Kasapis, who was the final editor for the initial manuscript.

TABLE OF CONTENTS

GENERALIZED ANXIETY DISORDER

Cognitive-Behavioral Therapy

❑ PRESENTING COMPLAINT

Terry is a 31-year-old man living in Washington, D.C. At his initial interview, he was dressed in clean but rather shabby "college clothes" (a T-shirt, jeans, and an old, worn warm-up jacket). Terry's manner and posture revealed that he was very apprehensive about therapy; his eyes nervously scanned the interview room, he held himself stiffly rigid and stayed by the door, and his speech was barely audible and marked by hesitations and waverings. After some brief introductions Terry and the therapist each took a seat. The therapist began the session, asking, "What is it that brings you here today?"

Terry's reply was very rapid and forced. He stated that his problems began during his hospital internship after he graduated from medical school. His internship was a high-pressure position that involved a great many demands and responsibilities. The schedule—involving thirty-six-hour on-call periods, daily rounds, and constant emergencies—was arduous and exhausting. Gradually he began to notice that he and the other interns were making a number of small errors and oversights in the care they provided their patients. He found himself ruminating about these lapses, and he began to hesitate in making decisions and taking action for fear of making some catastrophic mistake. His anxieties about making a mistake worsened until he began calling in sick and avoiding particularly stressful situations at the hospital. As a result he was not completing many of the assignments given to him by the chief resident of his program, who threatened to report him to the head of the program. As the year wore on Terry's performance continued to decline, and by the end of the year he was threatened with dismissal from the program. He resigned at the end of the year.

Before his resignation he began making plans to be transferred to a less demanding program. With some help from his father (who was a physician) and some luck, he was accepted into a program in Washington, D.C. This internship was indeed less demanding than the first, and he felt that perhaps he could manage it. After a few months, though, Terry again felt over-whelmed by his recurrent anxieties about making a terrible mistake. He had to quit the second program after six months. He then began to work in a less stressful position as a research fellow for the National Institutes of Health. Even in this relatively relaxed atmosphere, Terry found that he still had great difficulty carrying out his duties. He found that he could not handle any negative feelings at work, and he again began missing work to avoid trouble. Terry's contract with the FDA expired after six months; it was not renewed. At this time even the prospect of having to apply for another position produced terrible anxieties, and Terry decided to live off a trust fund set up by his grandfather, instead of working. For the last two years he has been supported by this trust fund and, in part at least, by his girlfriend, with whom he lives and who, according to Terry, pays "more than her share."

Terry's incapacitating anxieties have interfered not only with his career, but also with his relationships with his family and his girlfriend. As one indication of this, he has avoided visiting his parents for the last three years. He states that his parents' (particularly his father's) poor opinion of him make going home "out of the question." He also confesses that he avoids discussing any potentially controversial subject with his girlfriend for fear that he may cause an irreconcilable rift. As Terry puts it, "I stay away from anything touchy because I don't want to say something wrong and blow it (the relationship). Then what'll I do?" Even routine tasks—such as washing his clothes, shopping for groceries, and writing letters to friends—are impossible to accomplish for fear that some small step may be bungled or overlooked. Terry freely acknowledges that his fears are exaggerated and irrational. He admits (after some persuasion) that he is an intelligent, capable young man. Nevertheless, he feels utterly unable to overcome his anxieties, and he takes great pains to avoid situations that may potentially bring them on.

Along with these dysfunctional cognitions, Terry reports a number of somatic symptoms. He is very tense; he always feels nervous or "keyed up" and is easily distracted and irritated by minor problems. He complains of frequent throbbing headaches, annoying body aches and pains (especially in his back and neck), and an almost constant feeling of fatigue. He also admits to feeling worthless, and he describes himself as having low self-esteem and little motivation. Occasionally he also experiences brief periods of panic in which he suffers from shortness of breath, a wildly racing heartbeat, perfuse sweating, and mild dizziness. These feelings of panic tend to come on when some feared situation (e.g., having to make a decision or having to confront his girlfriend) cannot be avoided. He states that these symptoms initially emerged during his first internship and have gradually intensified over the past few years.

Terry began psychodynamic therapy soon after he lost his job with the FDA and stopped working. He reports that this therapy was very complex and involving. In particular, he says that his therapeutic experience gave him two important insights into the underlying causes of his paralyzing anxieties and his low self-esteem: (1) his parents' expectations of him were too high, and he always felt a great pressure to be perfect in their eyes; and (2) the teasing he received from his peers as a child has made him self-conscious of his weaknesses. Although Terry felt that these insights were valid, they did not seem to precipitate any significant change in his behavior, and they were becoming less useful to him. In his words, "the effect of these (insights) was wearing off." A friend suggested that Terry might benefit from a more direct form of psychotherapy and referred him to a cognitive-behavior therapist.

☐ PERSONAL HISTORY

Terry grew up in a small town in Ohio. His father is a general practitioner in town and is on the staff of the county hospital. Terry's mother is a teacher. She quit her job when his older sister was born. After his younger sister was diagnosed as mentally retarded, however, she returned to school to acquire special training in teaching handicapped children. She now teaches learning-disabled children as part of the county special education program. Terry's parents, particularly his father, always had high aspirations for him and were quite demanding.

Terry's older sister still lives with her parents and attends a small, little-known law school near home. Terry describes her as "not too bright." He states that his father is frustrated at being stuck in a small town and criticizes his daughter for not getting into a more prestigious law school. His younger sister is moderately mentally retarded. She too lives at home, and she works at a sheltered workshop run by the county special education program.

Terry always had the impression that he was looked on as the "success" of the family. He had always gotten excellent grades in school; in fact he won full scholarships that supported both his undergraduate education and his training in medical school, both at highly prestigious universities. He had always considered himself to be a very good student. He enjoyed studying, even in the difficult atmosphere of medical school. He described his academic achievement as something he did for himself—for his own education and improvement. In contrast, during his internship he felt that he was toiling endlessly on what he considered to be "someone else's scum work." For the first time he began to fear his own fallibility and to avoid anxiety-provoking situations.

☐ CONCEPTUALIZATION AND TREATMENT

Terry is a very intelligent and articulate young man, and he appears to be much more competent and able than he describes. He shows no evidence of a psychotic disorder. He seems willing, even pressured, to discuss his problems, and he seems highly motivated toward reducing them. The therapist thought it reasonable, then, to take Terry's complaints at face value.

Terry's primary problem involves his excessive and unwarranted apprehension about his own fallibility and his need to perform every activity, no matter how trivial, perfectly. This overriding fear has crippled his occupational and social functioning as well as his ability to perform—or even to attempt—a variety of routine, everyday tasks. This anxiety is also manifested by a number of physiological symptoms, including constant vigilance, distractibility, and irritability; pervasive muscle tension; and autonomic hyperactivity (as expressed by his occasional feelings of panic). Although he complains of periods of feeling depressed and worthless, his worries and anxieties are clearly not limited to these periods. Thus it seems that his anxiety is his primary problem and not merely a response to his mild depression.

Terry's symptoms clearly fit the *DSM-III-R* criteria for Generalized Anxiety Disorder. People with this disorder suffer from pervasive feelings of dread or worry that involve at least two or more major life circumstances (one's career, one's relationship with a spouse, the health of one's children, etc.). The focus of these anxieties is much more broad and unspecified than is the case with other anxiety disorders such as Panic Disorder or Simple Phobia. Furthermore, these feelings of anxiety are not solely associated with any other Axis I diagnosis. Thus, for example, although someone with Generalized Anxiety Disorder may also experience a Major Depressive Episode, his or her anxieties are not solely about being depressed. In addition, people with Generalized Anxiety Disorder display somatic signs of their apprehension, including motor tension, autonomic hyperactivity, and defensive vigilance.

Terry's therapy can be organized as a process involving four general steps. The therapist's initial aim was to establish rapport with her client. In order to establish a better working relationship with Terry, she attempted to make him feel comfortable with her, and she carefully explained her approach. Since cognitive-behavioral therapy requires much more direct, active participation than many clients suppose (particularly those with a history of psychodynamic treatment), it is important that the client be fully aware of what to expect. The therapist also gave Terry encouragement that his disorder was treatable with cognitive-behavioral therapy. It is important to establish this basis of hope in order to foster the client's expectations for change.

The second step was to have Terry form goals for his therapy. Ideally these goals would involve some specific behavior or attitude. Concrete plans that address some specific feared situation, such as "I want to send my resume to 50 prospective employers," are more effective than more general aims, such as "I want to work." Like most clients, though, Terry's initial goals were quite vague and unfocused. He stated that he wanted to start working, to get along with his parents better, and to "be not so apprehensive about things." At first these general goals are adequate; the important point is to have the client formulate *some* goals. Overly general ones can always be specified and put into behavioral contexts as therapy progresses.

Third, relaxation training is suggested for clients who show a great deal of physical tension and seem amenable to this treatment. Therapists have developed relaxation techniques that specifically address a client's dysfunctional cognitions, muscular tension, and autonomic hyperactivity. When he began therapy, Terry showed a variety of physical manifestations of tension. Having been trained in medicine, he was especially attuned to the somatic aspects of healing and was very willing to try relaxation techniques that involved physiological elements.

The fourth step in therapy was a review by Terry and the therapist of the issues and goals Terry had targeted. By going over his initial complaints and plans, both the therapist and the client are assured that they understand each other fully. In addition, this review allows the client, with the aid of the therapist, to put his or her initially vague goals into more specific and workable terms.

Therapy began with a discussion of the specific issues that were of immediate concern to Terry. These topics were not necessarily a central part of Terry's goals, nor were they necessarily closely related. For example, Terry's first few sessions of therapy focused on several distinct problems including, among other things, his inability to buy a suit, his anxiety concerning needed dental work, and his dread of an upcoming visit to his parents. These loosely related issues were dealt with on a problem-by-problem basis, a process the therapist referred to as "putting out fires." This troubleshooting approach is employed for several reasons. First, cognitive-behavioral therapy is most effective if therapeutic issues are specified and well defined; individual psychological "fires" are particularly suited to this. Second, the client's enthusiasm for therapy and belief in the effectiveness of treatment is likely to be increased by initial success experiences, especially in immediate problem areas. Third, although these issues do not appear to be closely related, for the most part they share a common foundation: they are indications of Terry's tendency to avoid situations that carry a possibility of failure, however slight. Over time, clients are expected to integrate these isolated issues and apply their therapeutic gains to other areas of their lives.

The first topic Terry wanted to discuss was his inability to buy himself a suit. It had been years since Terry had shopped for clothes; he contented himself with wearing worn jeans and T-shirts. Terry's girlfriend was making plans for the two of them to take a vacation to Boston to visit her sister. As part of the preparation for this trip, she had asked him to buy some new clothes, including "at least one decent suit." He had thought about buying a suit on several previous occasions, but every time the prospect of having to pick one out overwhelmed him. He would begin shaking and sweating even as he approached a clothing store. Terry explained that he hated shopping for clothes, especially suits, because he was convinced that he would not be able to pick out the right suit. In order to be at all acceptable, the suit had to be just the right color, just the right material, just the right cut, just the right price. It also had to be practical—appropriate for every possible occasion, from sightseeing to going to the symphony. The threat of making a mistake and buying "the wrong suit" made him so anxious that he could not bring himself even to enter a clothing store.

The therapist began by having Terry clarify exactly what he was and was not capable of. She then gave him clear assignments that she judged he would be able to accomplish successfully. These assignments started off with small steps that would be easy for Terry, and gradually became more and more complicated and difficult. The following segment of a therapy session illustrates this process:

> **Terry:** You see, I just can't go through with it (buying a suit).
>
> **Therapist:** Do you mean you actually are unable to, or that you'd rather avoid the whole thing?

Terry: What do you mean?

Therapist: Well, if I held a gun to your head, would you be able to go to the clothing store?

Terry: Well, yeah, I suppose so.

Therapist: So you are physically able to walk into a clothing store, right?

Terry: Yeah, I guess I am.

Therapist: OK. I want you to go to at least two clothing stores on your way home today. All right?

Terry: The mall's too far away. I couldn't possibly make it today.

Therapist: There's no need to go to the mall. There are at least five good clothing stores right around here; three are on this street.

Terry: Well, they're too expensive.

Therapist: No, not really. I've shopped at most of them, and the prices are actually better than at the mall.

Terry: I really don't know if I'll have the time . . .

Therapist: It'll take a half an hour at most. Come on, Terry, no more excuses. I want you to go to two stores. Today.

Terry: But what if I buy the wrong suit?

Therapist: You don't need to actually buy anything. Just walk into two stores. If you feel comfortable with that, then start browsing. You might want to try one or two suits on. But for today, I just want you to take the first step and go to two stores. Agreed?

Terry: All right.

At the next session Terry was noticeably excited and pleased. He had followed the therapist's directions and had gone to a store. After he got to the first one, he found that looking for a suit was not as difficult as he had expected. In fact, he actually went to three stores and even bought two suits. Unfortunately Terry was not able to enjoy his success for long; his enthusiasm evaporated when he began to describe another problem. Terry's driver's license had expired several weeks ago. He felt very anxious about driving with his expired license, and he knew that he had to get his license renewed, which involved taking a simple written test of basic traffic regulations. He got a copy of the driver's manual and planned to go over it several times, but each time he was struck with a terrible fear that he might miss some vital piece of information and fail his test. Terry admitted that his worries were irrational. He had taken similar written tests three times before and had only missed one or two questions in total. He realized that the test was very basic and that the chances of him actually failing the test were remote, even if he did not study the manual at all. Still, he could not bring himself to study the manual, and the thought of taking the test "cold" terrified him.

Again, the therapist approached the problem directly and made concrete suggestions. First, she reassured him that he was a very intelligent person who would have no trouble passing the test. Next, she suggested different ways to get him to read the manual, such as skimming it or just reading every other page. She explained that failing the exam was not the end of the world; even on the slight chance that he did fail the exam, he would still have two other opportunities to retake it. Finally, she reminded him that it was worse to be stopped while driving with an expired license than just to go ahead and get his renewed. This last warning was meant to propel Terry to action; however, it could have been counterproductive in that it might have caused Terry to develop so much anxiety about driving that he might have given it up altogether. With this in mind, the therapist reassured Terry that driving with a license that had expired only a few weeks ago would most likely get him only a warning. At worst, he would have to pay a small fine. As time wore on, however, trying to explain that he "just forgot" about his license would become less and less credible.

Again Terry followed the therapist's instructions. He read over the manual carefully and tried not to be too concerned if he did not remember every fact. Following her directions, if he felt that he could not remember some information from any particular page, he would consciously limit himself to skimming that page once. As expected, he passed his test. In fact, he didn't miss a question. However, this accomplishment, like that of the previous week, was accompanied by another "emergency."

Over the weekend Terry had lost a filling in one of his teeth while eating some caramel candy. He realized that he needed his filling replaced, and his girlfriend had suggested her dentist, whom she recommended highly. Terry had not been to a dentist for over three years, and he was very apprehensive about the possible injury and pain a dentist could inflict. His most horrible fear was that the dentist (or any dentist, for that matter) might inadvertently damage the nerve of the tooth, thus necessitating root canal work. In spite of this fear, Terry had realized that he needed his filling replaced and called for an emergency appointment. He was able to make an appointment for Tuesday morning for a consultation.

Although hesitant, Terry was able to make it to the dentist's office, accompanied by his girlfriend. Once in the dentist's chair, however, he became panicky and unmanageable. He clenched his mouth and made it impossible for the dentist to examine it. He repeatedly grabbed the dentist's hand and tried to jerk it away. Terry's girlfriend, who stayed with him throughout the appointment, told him that he made a high-pitched whistling sound resembling a drill whenever the dentist picked up one of his tools—even tools totally unrelated to the drill, such as the probing pick or the suction tube. She had never seen him this nervous before. At first the dentist refused to schedule an appointment to fill the tooth, but Terry's girlfriend, who was a longtime patient, convinced him to schedule an appointment for the next week.

Terry was depressed over this embarrassing experience. The worst part of it, he thought, was that his girlfriend would lose interest in him now that she had seen how anxious he was about things as trivial as dental exams. But since she had been able to schedule the appointment, Terry felt that his first priority now was to learn to control his apprehensions about going to the dentist.

Terry's therapy that week focused on relaxation training. He was taught to begin by taking slow, deep breaths. After a few deep breaths, he was told to relax his body completely. He was instructed to focus on his bodily sensations. He was to move his focus slowly from head to toe, concentrating on relaxing each part of his body. He was to sense how his forehead felt, then his eyebrows, then his nose, and so on. If he noticed tension in any part of his body, he was instructed to relax it. (Many therapists have their clients consciously tense and then relax various parts of their bodies during this exercise. In her experience, however, Terry's therapist prefers to focus primarily on relaxing, because most clients with anxiety disorders are already extremely tense. She prefers to avoid any suggestion that may exacerbate their muscular tension.) Terry was also told that if he found himself becoming distracted or had any stray thoughts, he was to "blow them away like puffy clouds" and replace them with soft, relaxing images. The therapist then asked Terry about the activities that were particularly pleasant to him. He replied that he loved the tranquillity of lying in the sun on some tropical island. As a result, the therapist told him that he should try to replace any stressful thoughts with scenes of sunbathing on a Caribbean beach.

Terry was told to practice this relaxation technique two or three times a day. To get her clients to do this practice, Terry's therapist makes relaxation tapes that gently and calmly guide the client in the exercises. Each tape is made individually, using the client's name and giving instructions specially tailored for him or her. To help ensure that her clients do not lose interest in these relaxation exercises, the tapes are short—no more than ten to fifteen minutes. Because of his impending dental appointment, Terry's therapist made his tape right after their session. She also wrote out the rationale for not continuing to avoid the various things that he needed to accomplish and the role of relaxation in reducing his anxiety so that entering into these situations would be possible. He expressed gratitude for her effort and her personal concern when he picked these up the next morning.

Terry began the next session by proudly exclaiming, "I survived!" He reported that he used the relaxation training to divert his focus throughout the appointment, and this was very successful. (In fact he reported that he focused on his feet.) Terry's therapist, who herself had had a filling replaced just two months earlier, acknowledged that it was a stressful and difficult experience and that he should be congratulated on his accomplishment. During the session Terry reported that he had also used the relaxation training in a completely different situation. While he was having lunch with some friends, Terry began to feel that his friends were ignoring him. He became upset and irritated at them and began worrying that his companions were no longer interested in maintaining their friendship with him. Instead of leaving the restaurant, however, he decided to use the relaxation training to relieve his tension and to replace these negative anxieties with more pleasant images. As a result he was able to remain calm during lunch, which turned out to be a pleasant experience after all.

The next several sessions focused on different individual topics. For example, Terry had not done any laundry in over a year. He avoided this chore because he could not bring himself to go through the effort of sorting the clothes properly, making sure each load of clothes had the correct amount of detergent and was run under the right cycle, and so forth. He also dreaded folding the laundry—lining up each crease exactly and folding the T-shirts just right to avoid any wrinkles. Nevertheless, he wanted to surprise his girlfriend by doing their laundry, and he asked the therapist for her help. First, the task of doing the laundry was broken down into manageable subparts (sorting, selecting the cycle, etc.). Terry was then instructed to approach each subpart separately and to go on only if he felt calm and relaxed. He was also told that most people find that their first instincts are best, so once he made a decision about sorting or folding, he was to go through with it. Prior to starting, Terry wrote out careful instructions on exactly how to wash the clothes and put them away. It took Terry quite a while to accomplish this job, but he was able to control his anxieties and move steadily from subpart to subpart. When he reported completing the job at the next session, he was complimented and encouraged to attempt other avoided activities.

Another source of apprehension concerned writing a letter to an old roommate from college. He had not responded to this friend's last three or four letters for fear that he might make some mistake in his grammar or spelling. He worried that the friend, who was a journalist, would see this mistake and lose respect for him. Terry's anxieties were heightened after his friend's last letter. In it, the friend jokingly wondered whether Terry had forgotten how to write. This comment made Terry wonder if he had indeed lost his ability to compose a letter that would be acceptable to his friend. Like everything else, his therapist had Terry approach this problem in gradual steps. First he was to outline briefly what he would put in a letter. Next, he was to write a letter that they could go over during the next session. As was the case with shopping for a suit, renewing his license, and doing the laundry, Terry found that just starting an avoided activity greatly diminished his apprehensions, and he finished and sent the letter without ever showing it to the therapist.

Terry found that his anxieties diminished more quickly and that he required fewer steps to complete the task after each "fire" was put out. After several sessions of "putting out fires," Terry's therapy began to focus on more global interpersonal issues. At one session, Terry discussed his fears that his girlfriend was planning to leave him. During the previous week she had said that a special project had come up at work (she worked in an architectural firm) and that they would have to postpone their vacation to Boston for a month. Terry, who constantly harbored fears that she would end their relationship, took this as a sign that she was ready to leave. He asked the therapist what he could do to make her stay. The therapist told him that no one could guarantee their relationship would last forever, and she began to discuss whether it was likely that Terry's fears were accurate. Initially Terry refused to discuss this possibility, saying "Don't tell me anything about her leaving. I don't want to hear it." His therapist persisted, however, and reminded him of the importance of not avoiding important topics. Over the next two sessions he gradually became able to discuss the possibility of his girlfriend leaving him. He even made some plans if indeed this occurred. (As it turned out, she had been honest with him, and they went to Boston on the rescheduled date.)

While they were away, Terry's mother fell and broke her hip. This became the topic of discussion when he returned. Terry knew he was expected to visit her, but he dreaded going home and interacting with his parents, particularly his father. He said that his father was very demanding and would undoubtedly ask Terry about what he had been doing over the past few years. He pleaded with his therapist, "Tell me what to say."

The therapist engaged Terry in a role-playing exercise. First, she instructed him to enact his father while she modeled effective responses to the father's comments and criticisms. Terry was told to pay close attention while she modeled these behaviors; he was to remember such things as her gestures, the color of her blouse, and so on. Mostly these details were meant to give Terry a clear, visual reference that would help him remember the gist of the modeled responses. After going over several responses, the roles were changed. Now the therapist enacted the role of Terry's parents, and Terry discussed possible responses from his own viewpoint. Since it was felt that maintaining a good interaction with his parents was just as important as dealing with a bad one, Terry practiced responding to many different types of comments, both positive and negative.

When Terry returned from Ohio, he reported that his father was indeed as critical as Terry had anticipated. His father was very disappointed that Terry had "thrown away" a career in medicine, and he kept asking Terry what he had been doing for the past three years. His father felt that every man should at least support himself by the time he was finished with his education. Although these interactions made Terry very anxious, he was able to stay in the family home for the entire visit (ten days). Terry stated that his interactions with his mother and older sister were generally positive. He found, somewhat to his surprise, that he really enjoyed their company. Although he still felt nervous about visiting his parents, he felt that he could have an adequate interaction with them and decided not to wait so long before visiting them again. (Although Terry was more comfortable about discussing his parents after six months of therapy, by this time he had still not actually visited them again.)

The next focus of therapy was for Terry to apply for jobs. Initially Terry seemed perfectly happy to continue living off the trust fund, even though he had reported "getting back to work" as a goal of therapy. He now admitted that his father had a point: Terry was 31, and he should begin to support himself. In addition, his therapist reminded him that the trust fund would not last forever. She also noted that the longer he waited before he started working again, the harder it would be to explain the ever-increasing gap in his resume.

Like every other aspect of therapy, Terry and his therapist approached this task one step at a time. First, they discussed the sorts of jobs he would be interested in and capable of performing. (Terry's estimations of his own abilities were consistently lower than those of his therapist.) Also, he wanted to avoid any job that involved pressure and responsibility. At first, he thought of becoming a library researcher for some government agency. His therapist, who also thought it wise to avoid any high-pressure positions, told him that he could probably do better, perhaps something that would enable him to use his medical training. They finally decided that he should seek employment that involved medical issues but was outside a hospital or clinic setting. The therapist's instructions were concrete and firm: by the next week he was to have his resume compiled, and one week later he was to have it printed. She then directed him to send out at least ten applications per week until he heard something. During this time they rehearsed possible interview questions through role-playing. After eight weeks (and by making use of a few old contacts), he was offered a part-time position at the Food and Drug

Administration as a research assistant. He found that he enjoyed working and could do his job well. After six months he was offered a full-time staff position.

Terry discontinued therapy at about the time that he was hired full-time. His therapy had involved an eight-month process of directly approaching various psychological "fires" and learning to cope with his fears. With these success experiences, he was slowly able to develop a sense of himself that was more in line with his actual abilities. He reported that over the past few months his self-esteem had gradually improved and his risk-avoidance habits were starting to decline. He still worried about performing various tasks and duties well, but he was now able to attempt these activities in spite of his apprehensions. Only rarely did his fears cause him to avoid these situations. He was able to discuss possible negative consequences of his own and other people's actions. In short, although he stated that he still felt anxious about some situations, he felt that he was learning to control his fears. He felt better about himself and his work. Most noticeably, he was working steadily and engaging routinely in a wide variety of activities that he would not even have attempted just six months earlier.

☐ PROGNOSIS

Terry's prognosis is excellent. When he began therapy, he had very low self-esteem and very little confidence in his abilities to perform even the most trivial task adequately. Consequently he avoided situations that involved any amount of pressure or responsibility. His constant fears of being embarrassed or rejected also interfered with his interpersonal relationships. Without treatment, it is possible that Terry would have become severely agoraphobic; that is, so overwhelmed by his anxieties that he would be unable to leave his home or interact with other people. At the very least, it is likely that his ability to carry out his day-to-day tasks and his ability to maintain his relationships with his family, friends, and girlfriend would have continued to deteriorate.

Terry has reversed this trend. His paralyzing anxieties are greatly diminished, and his avoidance behavior has for the most part ended. By approaching feared situations directly and in small increments, Terry's therapy seems gradually to have enabled him to approach a variety of previously avoided situations. In addition, he is able to apply this step-by-step approach, and the relaxation training he received, to problem areas that were never directly discussed in therapy. He also seems to have been able to integrate the therapeutic gains of these isolated tasks and make progress in more global problems involving his interpersonal relationships and his career. In addition to his behavioral gains, Terry has also built up his self-esteem and self-confidence, as evidenced by a shift in his therapy goals. Initially Terry's aim in therapy was to avoid any pain, rejection, or pressure in his career or his interpersonal relationships. Now, however, his goal is to attempt to work through difficult tasks and to avoid situations only if they may be unduly stressful. This shift appears to be a good indication that Terry will maintain his therapeutic gains.

☐ DISCUSSION

Terry's presenting complaints contain elements that may indicate the presence of a number of different anxiety disorders. For example, Terry's refusal to engage in everyday tasks for fear of being ridiculed may be taken as evidence of a Social Phobia (a strict avoidance of potentially embarrassing or humiliating situations). However, Terry also fears a variety of situations that have no obvious evaluative component (e.g., washing his clothes), and he seems to be more apprehensive about his own and others' possible failures than about the negative evaluations of these failures. Similarly, Terry's panicky feelings and obsessive thoughts about his fallibility may indicate the presence of Panic Disorder or possibly Obsessive-Compulsive Disorder. However, these symptoms are not sufficiently marked to fulfill the *DSM-III-R* criteria for these diagnoses. Like most people with an anxiety disorder, Terry displays a variety of anxious symptoms. In these cases the therapist must take care to determine the appropriate diagnosis for each case. Although Terry manifests symptoms that suggest several different anxiety disorders, the most appropriate diagnosis for him is Generalized Anxiety Disorder.

In addition to his anxiety disorder, Terry's attitudes seem to reflect an underlying Obsessive-Compulsive Personality Disorder. His perfectionism, his preoccupation with details, his indecisiveness, and his conviction that other people are incompetent all indicate the presence of this personality disorder. In fact, it could be said that Terry's anxiety disorder first emerged when he became overwhelmed by these obsessive characteristics. Depressive symptoms are also a common associated feature of anxiety disorders. (Some therapists have noted that the focus of people's dysfunctional attitudes often dictates whether they will show primarily depressed or anxious symptoms. Specifically, people who focus on past negative events tend to be depressed, whereas those who focus on future negative events tend to be anxious.)

There are two atypical features in this case. First, most people diagnosed with Generalized Anxiety Disorder suffer from diffuse, vaguely formed anxiety; they are rarely able to identify the source of their pervasive worries.

Terry's fears, on the other hand, seem to be organized around issues clearly associated with his obsessive-compulsive traits. In fact, this type of obsessive thinking occurs in only a small minority of cases.

Second, Generalized Anxiety Disorder rarely becomes so thoroughly crippling. Most clients with this disorder report feeling "unhappy" or "uncomfortable" with their lives, and some suffer some minor disruption of their occupational or interpersonal functioning or both (e.g., they may be passed over for promotion because of their indecisiveness or their tendency to hesitate, their spouses may become irritated by their constant fears and worries, etc.). However, most people with an anxiety disorder are quite productive; when they do fail, their anxiety is usually not the direct cause. In contrast, in the course of a few years Terry had stopped working completely and was on the verge of becoming a total recluse. He was unable to complete even the simplest everyday tasks. In his therapist's words, "Terry didn't just suffer from severe anxiety, he really wasn't living a life." With the exception of those who are severely agoraphobic or obsessive-compulsive, it is very unlikely that people's apprehensions would make them give up their career and their relationships.

Cognitive-behavioral therapy is quite different from more traditional psychodynamic therapies. Most cognitive-behavioral therapists have little interest in their clients' family histories or in their interpretations of past events, and consequently the histories they obtain tend to be limited to objective, factual information—such as the chronology of the person's symptoms and the situations that seem to exacerbate these symptoms. Instead of investigating their clients' early traumas and dynamic interpretations of events, they take a more active role in directly modifying their clients' actual behaviors. That is, a client's specific complaints are not considered superficial or defensive but are usually taken at face value; seemingly minor, specific problems (e.g., "I can't buy myself a suit") are considered part of the "real problem" and are addressed directly. Eventually, the treatment of these individual concerns will be incorporated into a coherent therapy package that the person can apply to other life situations.

Like Terry, most people who enter a direct form of therapy such as cognitive-behavioral treatment specifically seek out this form of therapy, often after they become frustrated with the slow progress of more traditional psychodynamic therapies. Sometimes such people have read about these more direct therapies, and sometimes, as in Terry's case, a friend will recommend it. Thus a person's decision to engage in cognitive-behavioral therapy is usually a conscious choice; it is rare that a person who is seeking psychodynamic therapy accidentally finds him- or herself in cognitive-behavioral therapy.

Often this direct perspective is exactly what the clients are seeking. In other cases, though, they become very uncomfortable with this approach.

They feel that direct therapy is too "trivial" or "superficial," and they fear that they will never get to the "real problem." Most therapists feel strongly that a client's beliefs about the effectiveness of therapy are an important part of the therapy, and as a result some therapists will refer such clients to psychodynamic therapists. Most, however, will attempt to convince the client that with time and effort the direct approach really does work.

MULTIPLE PERSONALITY DISORDER

Psychotherapy with Hypnosis*

❏ PRESENTING COMPLAINT

Sherry is a 28-year-old nurse's aide who has received inpatient psychiatric care off and on for the past five years. Approximately two weeks after her most recent readmission, she became very confused about her surroundings and complained that "everything had changed." She demanded to know who had rearranged the hospital and the grounds, and she repeatedly asked to see people who didn't exist, both patients and staff members. When staff members attempted to calm her down, she became verbally and physically abusive, shouting obscenities and swinging her fists.

Sherry had been admitted with a diagnosis of Schizophrenia, Disorganized Type, and to some therapists her strange and irrational behavior was evidence of yet another psychotic episode. Other therapists, however, believed that Sherry's behavior might be evidence of a dissociative state, a state of consciousness where one part of awareness is split off from another. In this case, it seemed that Sherry might have split off her memories from her waking self, and that her irrational behavior might be only the result of the conflict between her expectations and her perceptions. Sherry was given the Hypnotic Induction Profile (HIP) and was found to be highly hypnotizable,

17

scoring a 4–5 out of a possible 5. While in a hypnotic trance, she gave the present date as being eight months earlier than it in fact was and stated that she was at a hospital over a thousand miles away. The date she gave and her description of the hospital corresponded to a clinic she had attended just prior to her most recent admission. The therapist who hypnotized her found that Sherry had no memory of anything after leaving this clinic; it was as if she had lost the last eight months of her life. Clearly her "psychotic" behavior was actually the result of an amnesic period, not delusional ideation (see Case 7). Through hypnosis, Sherry was able to experience age regression (a reliving of the past as though it were the present) to the time of her earlier hospitalization. During this session involving age regression, she was able to recognize her present surroundings as different from her "regressed" world, and she was able to reorient herself to her present time and location. With the establishment of her diagnosis as a dissociative disorder, not a psychotic disorder, Sherry was taken off antipsychotic medication, and an intensive program of psychotherapy with hypnosis commenced.

Amnesic periods were not new to Sherry; she frequently complained of episodes of which she had no memory. Sherry, who is usually a quiet, demure, and conscientious person, reported being very frightened and concerned about these blackouts, since in the past such episodes seemed to involve "wild" behavior. According to the reports of her friends, family, and past therapists, she was hostile, angry, and self-destructive at such times. She would often notice that she had new cuts and bruises after a blackout, and on several occasions she woke up to find herself in bed with a strange man. For Sherry, the knowledge that she could not control her own behavior was very frightening.

Sherry's therapist, a psychiatrist who specialized in treating dissociative disorders, felt that the chances were good that Sherry suffered from Multiple Personality Disorder; she was highly hypnotizable, she had frequent amnesic periods, and her behavior during these periods was reported to be very different from her usual manner. The therapist decided to find out what happened to Sherry during her blackout periods.

Under hypnosis, Sherry experienced age regression back three weeks to the time of a recent amnesic episode. After a minute or so, while in a deep hypnotic trance, she suddenly looked up at the therapist and yelled, "What the hell do you want?" Her voice and tone had changed completely from the shy woman who had gone into the hypnotic trance. The therapist was somewhat startled by Sherry's sudden change in tone, and asked Sherry who she was. The patient, who was now clearly hostile, angry, and sarcastic, identified herself as Karla. Karla, who was somewhat irritated at the intrusion on her time, began a conversation with the therapist, who asked her what happened during the present amnesic episode (that is, the one that occurred three weeks ago). Karla explained that she had just picked up a man at a bar with the intention of going back to his apartment. She complained that Sherry had spoiled her fun by crying at the bar, causing the man to lose interest. Determined to punish Sherry, Karla threatened to inflict a deep cut on Sherry's leg. With intense hatred and bitterness, Karla ran an imaginary knife over a real scar on her leg, shouting, "Where's my knife? I'll show her; I'll really cut her this time! I'll go to sleep and let her find it!" She then closed her eyes. When her eyes reopened, her voice and manner were those of Sherry. Sherry gently touched the wound and sobbed quietly. When the therapist asked her how she got this cut, she appeared to be confused and hesitantly replied, "Well, I . . . I guess I was running in a field and fell; that's how I cut it."

☐ PERSONAL HISTORY

Sherry had a twin sister. They suffered numerous episodes of physical abuse and neglect throughout childhood. On one occasion, the mother bloodied Sherry's nose, and on another she broke Sherry's tooth with her fist. Both of these events occurred before Sherry was 4 years old. Sherry's mother also threw a pot of boiling water at her in a fit of rage, leaving her with second-degree burns on her arms and chest. After a bitter marriage lasting five years, her parents divorced. Two years later her mother remarried. Unfortunately for the twins, Sherry's stepfather was also violent; as his primary form of punishment he would beat the twins using a board with nails in it. After three or four years Sherry and her sister moved in with their biological father. Although he was more caring, he was nevertheless capable of abuse. For example, he would often beat the twin girls with a belt buckle during alcholic rages. After several years, Sherry's mother obtained a court order that gave her custody of the children. Immediately after winning custody, however, she sent the twins off to live at a strict military boarding school. After a few years at the boarding school, Sherry was separated from her sister.

For most of her life, Sherry had reduced the anxiety of this abuse and neglect by dissociating the traumas onto her sister. That is, she frequently experienced her physical and psychological pain as having happened to her twin sister, not to her. For example, Sherry stated that her mother once threw boiling water on her sister. However, her mother's and sister's testimony, as well as her medical records, show that in actuality Sherry was the one who was scalded as a child. It was not until she was separated from her sister, however, that she began to experience uncontrollable amnesic periods.

After her return from the boarding school, Sherry joined the army in hopes of being trained as a nurse. During this time she began to notice that there were long periods for which she had no memory. Her behavior during these periods was reported to be wild and unpredictable. She would often begin violent arguments with other recruits, and on several occasions she had sexual relations with male soldiers on the base or with strange men she would pick up at a bar. Although Sherry had no recollection of these actions, she would often find physical evidence (e.g., cuts and bruises, slips of paper with strange phone numbers, waking up in bed with a strange man, etc.) that would corroborate others' stories. She also made several suicidal gestures during her amnesic episodes, usually in the form of cutting herself on the forearms or taking an overdose of tranquilizers, or both. In addition, she had gone to the camp infirmary on several occasions and complained of auditory hallucinations and depression. As a result of her bizarre and disruptive behavior, Sherry received a psychiatric discharge and was hospitalized with a diagnosis of Schizophrenia, Disorganized Type (see Case 7). While in the hospital she was given antipsychotic medication, which did not seem to relieve her symptoms to any significant degree.

Sherry was admitted to several different psychiatric institutions over the next five years. At different times she was diagnosed as suffering from Bipolar Disorder, Major Depression, Schizophrenia, and Borderline Personality Disorder. As a result she had been treated with lithium, antidepressants, and antipsychotic medication, all with little lasting effect.

❑ CONCEPTUALIZATION AND TREATMENT

Multiple Personality Disorder is a dissociative disorder characterized by the coexistence of two or more distinct and unique personalities, each with its own system of social relationships and behavior patterns. At any one time, only one personality tends to dominate the person's consciousness, and the shifts between these different personalities can be quite abrupt. This case provides a good example of this rare diagnosis. Two very different personalities (Sherry and Karla) completely controlled the patient's consciousness at different times, and the shifts between them were often sudden and unpredictable. The patient's strong dissociative capacity (evidenced by her high hypnotizability) and her history of childhood abuse and neglect are also common in patients with this disorder.

Of course, people with strong dissociative capacities do not necessarily suffer from a psychiatric disorder. Often they will utilize this skill to repress the memory of particularly painful emotional and physical traumas. In fact, since people who have dissociative experiences use them as a sort of emotional buffer, most will never feel the need to seek psychological treatment. In some cases, however, the dissociation processes themselves bring about intense anxiety because they become involuntary and uncontrollable. Blackout periods and reports of uncharacteristic behavior that cannot be remembered are indications of these involuntary dissociations. Finding themselves unable to control their behavior, these people are compelled to seek psychological help (either by their own fears or by the insistence of other people). This seems to be the case with Sherry.

In her case, the dissociative processes that helped her endure her painful childhood experiences may have led her to establish an alternate personality, Karla, who now causes her to behave in bizarre and disruptive ways. The primary goal of therapy with Sherry, then, is to harness her own dissociative powers (through self-hypnosis) in order to reexperience and better understand her childhood traumas. With this insight, she may gradually be able to diminish the frequency of her amnesic episodes and thereby gain control over her actions.

Sherry's therapy was organized into five stages. The first involved the establishment of a diagnosis of Multiple Personality Disorder with hysterical, psychotic, and depressive features. With this diagnosis her therapist was able to reconceptualize her symptoms as being the result of self-induced dissociated states, rather than a willful acting-out or an uncontrolled psychosis. He then discontinued her antipsychotic medication, which in any event did not seem to be effective. Using her hypnotizability as a therapeutic tool, the therapist attempted to provide structure to her spontaneous dissociative states through formal hypnosis. As therapy progressed, Sherry was gradually trained to gain a measure of control over her dissociative states through voluntarily induced self-hypnosis.

The second stage of psychotherapy involved setting limits on her self-destructive tendencies. Using self-hypnosis, she was taught to reexperience her past psychological traumas and learn not to blame herself for her past punishments. Sherry was also taught to express her emotions more openly, to prevent her hostility from being expressed through her dissociative states. On a more behavioral level, Sherry was frequently hospitalized for short periods to prevent her from carrying out her suicidal threats. In addition, antidepressant medication was administered to counteract her depressive symptoms.

The third stage of therapy focused on the transference between the patient and the therapist. Given Sherry's history of almost continuous abuse and neglect, it would have been difficult to expect her to trust her therapist fully and believe that he truly cared for her welfare. Instead, it is likely that she would have come to believe that her therapist was interested in her only because she was a fascinating case that would lend him prestige if he could cure her. In this light her frequent suicidal gestures were seen as tests of the therapist's commitment. Would he remain concerned for her welfare even at the risk of professional failure? At this stage it was essential for the therapist to face the possibility of failure as well as to maintain a clear interest in her well-being in spite of her suicidal gestures and her resistance to therapy. Above all, it was important for the therapist to be perceived as a supportive ally who would not abandon her.

The fourth (and perhaps the most crucial) stage of therapy was integrating the different personalities into one being. In order to accomplish this, Sherry first had to be convinced that the hostile and disruptive aspects of her subconscious were valuable and should not be suppressed. Indeed, her assertiveness and self-confidence were assets that should be incorporated into a more well-rounded personality. One technique that promoted this integration was giving "equal time" to both Sherry and Karla. In this way, Sherry could show her more aggressive emotions openly, thus reducing the need for Karla to rebel. Similarly, Karla was taught that Sherry's good-natured attributes could be quite useful in forming and maintaining relationships with others. Over a period of years, both personalities gradually incorporated elements of the other, and the shifts between them became smoother and less disruptive. After approximately four years of therapy, Sherry reported that she was aware of Karla for the first time. She described this realization as "like opening a door in myself." Karla then added, "I'm in here too. We're both here. It's not one or the other; we're together."

Another important aspect of this integration is to have the patient understand the traumatic memories and events that caused the dissociations in the first place. Furthermore, this must be done in a way that is acceptable to all aspects of his or her personality. However, the therapist must be cautious in this endeavor. On the one hand, pushing a patient to relive early traumas too quickly may exacerbate the dissociations. On the other hand, failing to deal with repressed traumas may perpetuate the need for dissociations in the future. In general, these patients are encouraged to confront and accept their painful memories, to gain control over these memories, and to restructure these memories in a way that is more consistent with their self-image.

In Sherry's case, her mother's persistent manipulation and neglect engendered strong feelings of guilt and obligation. Because her mother withheld love from Sherry for most of her childhood, Sherry became extremely dependent on her. One example of Sherry's feelings of obligation toward her mother is that she pays her mother's bills and provides her mother with a rent-free room in her apartment, this in spite of the fact that her mother is financially secure. (In fact, since Sherry has spent a great deal of the past ten years in psychiatric hospitals, her mother is much better off than Sherry is.) To add insult to injury, Sherry's mother does not appreciate this help; for example, in family therapy sessions the mother appeared to be much more interested in her vacation plans than in her daughter's improvement. Understandably, Sherry was very resentful of her mother's callous selfishness, yet she felt unable to challenge her directly. Instead she would criticize herself for being so weak and dependent. Often this self-derogation and repressed anger was expressed by Karla, who would cut Sherry's wrists or perform other acts of self-mutilation to punish Sherry for being so weak. Many times after paying her mother's bills, Sherry would emerge from the rest room with her arms dripping blood. She was saying to her mother symbolically what she couldn't say directly: "You are bleeding me to death." To prevent Sherry from venting her frustration in self-destructive ways in the future, Sherry's therapist urged her to ask her mother to pay her own bills and move out of the apartment. This confrontation was not without some cost; Sherry entered a severe depression after this episode. However, she responded well to antidepressant medication and began to function better after her recovery.

Finally, the fifth stage of Sherry's therapy involved interaction management as a means of helping her avoid the pathologic compliance and repressed resentment that characterized her previous relationships. Interaction management is a therapy technique used to teach the patient more effective ways of dealing with other people through the use of role-playing and modeling. As a part of this therapy, Sherry attended cojoint sessions with her mother, her sister, and her boyfriend. The therapist then provided Sherry with ways to react to the various interpersonal demands of these people more assertively.

The course of Sherry's therapy was very gradual. After four years of intensive inpatient and outpatient psychotherapy she was seen primarily on an outpatient basis. At this point the two personalities had recognized each other, and she began a relationship with a man. Her outpatient therapy, which took the form of frequent office consultations and occasional active interventions, continued for two years. During this time Sherry broke up with her boyfriend, and she entered a severe depression. However, she made no serious suicide attempts. She was given antidepressant medication and was able to remain an outpatient. Approximately three years later Sherry was raped. At that time she was brought to the hospital in a confused and agitated state. Hypnotic regression enabled her to relive the painful events of the rape and to convince herself that she was not responsible for the trauma. She was released from the hospital after only two weeks. For the past few years Sherry has received supportive psychotherapy off and on at her own request.

❑ PROGNOSIS

Sherry has made steady progress since beginning psychotherapy. Over the course of several years, her uncontrolled bursts of anger and self-mutilating behaviors have for the most part ceased, she has developed a more equitable relationship with her mother, and her therapy has progressed from inpatient care to outpatient care to intermittent support sessions. However, her extensive dissociative capacity leaves her vulnerable to future dissociative episodes in response to severe stress, particularly if it involves sexual or financial exploitation. An example of this vulnerability was evidenced after her rape. Although Sherry had been in psychotherapy for approximately eight years, she nevertheless suffered from uncontrollable dissociations as a result of this painful trauma.

Sherry's power to dissociate is a two-edged sword. While her ability to separate and repress the traumatic events of her life may insulate her from severely painful experiences, it may also leave her open to uncontrollable dissociations that frequently result in self-damaging acts or unacceptable behavior. Sherry's continued adjustment will depend on her ability to learn to use her powers of self-hypnosis to gain mastery over her intrapsychic processes. In summary, although the prognosis for Sherry is generally good, her therapist remains cautious about her ability to cope with painful, traumatic experiences independently. It remains to be seen whether Sherry will be able to completely control her dissociations in the face of severe life pressures.

☐ DISCUSSION

Most people with Multiple Personality Disorder, known as "multiples," share a number of common characteristics. First, most patients who suffer from dissociative disorders such as Multiple Personality Disorder, Psychogenic Amnesia, or Psychogenic Fugue (assuming a new identity and, in some cases, traveling to a different location) are highly hypnotizable. This ability is seen as fundamental in their tendency to develop a dissociative disorder, and it is used by some therapists as an instrumental part of their treatment. Second, the majority of people diagnosed with Multiple Personality Disorder report having suffered numerous severe traumas during childhood. It is thought that these early experiences may lead such people to develop a dissociative ability as a way of escaping these painful traumas, or at least isolating them from conscious awareness. A related point is that multiples typically develop elaborate fantasy worlds during childhood. These worlds often contain imaginary playmates who may share the child's pain. In Sherry's case, her twin sister may have fulfilled this role, as evidenced by Sherry's frequent confusions over whether she or her sister was actually the victim of various abuses during their childhood.

In addition to these global characteristics, the different personalities of most multiples are organized in characteristic ways. Roughly speaking, these personalities form three basic clusters: the so-called "core personality," aggressive personalities, and intermediary personalities. The core personality (or in some cases core personalities) is the individual commonly known to most people. This personality is usually quiet, meek, and obedient, with a primary aim of pleasing others and avoiding pain.

A second cluster consists of one or more personalities that are self-confident, outgoing, and assertive. Often these personalities become aggressive or reckless. One of the primary functions of these personalities appears to be expressing hostile or aggressive emotions that the core personality finds unacceptable. Many times these personalities attack the people who have mistreated them in their lives (e.g., abusive or exploitive parents, spouses, or bosses), but usually their anger is directed toward the core personality. Sometimes they may attempt to punish the core personality for its weakness through suicide attempts or by inflicting painful wounds. At other times these aggressive personalities may take advantage of the core personality in more subtle ways. In one case, a man's aggressive personality wrecked a car the core personality had borrowed from a friend. Subsequently, this second personality let the core personality "wake up" at the scene of the accident to explain the wreck to the police and the owner.

A third cluster includes personalities that act as intermediaries between the submissive and aggressive personalities. Often the function of these personalities is to reconcile the different needs and concerns of the others. They also seem to function as rational spokespersons who can handle pressure and explain the wild and disruptive actions of the aggressive personalities. As therapy progresses, most multiples show evidence of personalities that fit each of the clusters. Therapists using hypnosis find it helpful to make use of a personality from the third, intermediary cluster of personalities at the beginning stages of therapy. This personality tends to be fully aware of the actions of all the other personalities, and it is relatively receptive to treatment.

The present case is somewhat unusual in that only two distinct personalities, Sherry and Karla, emerged. However, these two personalities clearly fit the first two clusters just described.

The interactions among the different personalities have two common properties. First, these interactions are characterized by "asymmetric amnesia." Typically the core personality has no direct knowledge of the other personalities, whereas these other personalities have at least a limited knowledge of the others. In most cases at least one personality (typically an intermediary personality) is omniscient; this personality becomes the focus of therapeutic attempts at integration. In this case Karla knew all about Sherry—her thoughts and feelings as well as her actions. In contrast, Sherry experienced amnesic periods when Karla took over. She knew nothing about

Karla's existence except for physical signs Karla would leave (e.g., a wound) or from the reports of other people. Although Karla was a rather hostile personality who was somewhat difficult to work with, she nevertheless provided the therapist with the best pathway toward integration.

A second characteristic of the interaction between personalities is "trance logic," a suspension of the rules of logic and reason. A common scenario involving trance logic concerns an aggressive personality's attempts to harm the core personality. The following example is taken from the case of Sherry. After a suicide attempt the therapist asked to speak to Karla. When she appeared, he asked her if she was worried about what would happen to her if Sherry actually died. Karla responded, "It doesn't matter. I could just float to some other body. But for now I've got to be with her."

One difficulty in accurately diagnosing Multiple Personality Disorder is that it shares many features with other diagnoses. The hostile, disruptive, and uncontrolled behaviors of the aggressive personality may indicate Oppositional Disorder, Antisocial Personality Disorder, or Borderline Personality Disorder. The frequent depressed behavior and suicidal attempts understandably lead many therapists to a diagnosis of Major Depression. In some cases, the aggressive personality is so uncontrolled and delusional that a diagnosis of Schizophrenia or Paranoid Disorder is indicated. Clearly establishing these psychotic and depressive symptoms as resulting from a dissociation is not an easy task, and a proper diagnosis is greatly facilitated by a therapist who is experienced in recognizing and treating dissociative disorders. These therapists tend to have special training in techniques involving hypnosis. In the past, many therapists were skeptical of hypnosis as a legitimate adjunct to treatment. As the acceptance of hypnosis increases, however, so does the number of patients diagnosed as having this disorder. At the present time it is unclear whether this growth merely reflects an increased awareness of Multiple Personality Disorder or an actual increase in its incidence.

---

*Many of the descriptions in this case are based on material from the following sources: Spiegel, D. (1986). Dissociating damage. *American Journal of Clinical Hypnosis, 29*, 123-131; Spiegel, D. & Fink, R. (1979). Hysterical psychosis and hypnotizability. *American Journal of Psychiatry, 136*, 777-781.

DEPENDENT PERSONALITY DISORDER

Sociocultural Humanistic Therapy

❏ PRESENTING COMPLAINT

Kathy telephoned the outpatient psychiatry clinic desperate for help. Over the last few years she had become increasingly frustrated with her life. She felt manipulated at her job and dissatisfied with her "ugly face and fat body." However, clearly the most distressing aspect of her life was that recently she had become convinced that her marriage of three years' duration was falling apart. Her primary complaints about her marriage focused on three interrelated issues: (1) her husband's failure to pay adequate attention to her, (2) her perception that her husband was constantly attempting to seduce other women, and (3) her own jealous and bitter reactions to his behavior. Since Kathy's complaints centered on her relationship with her husband, Tom, she was encouraged to enlist his cooperation in couple therapy. Tom reluctantly agreed, saying that he did so "for Kathy's sake."

At their first session Kathy and Tom presented themselves as a successful young couple. Both partners appeared to be highly intelligent, friendly, and socially active—this last characteristic was especially true of Tom. However, both partners seemed somewhat superficial, being overly preoccupied with their physical appearance and social activities. Contrary to her self-descriptions during her initial telephone call, Kathy, 29, was intelligent and attractive. She held a bachelor's degree in biology and worked as a consultant for the Florida State Water Commission. In addition, she taught aerobics at a local health club and occasionally modeled for an agency in Tampa, Florida, where they lived. Although she was successful in a scientific career and in modeling, Kathy described herself in critical terms. For instance, when she made minor mistakes, such as forgetting an item on a grocery list, she would demean herself by calling herself "spacey" or "just an airhead." She was also continually dissatisfied with her physical appearance, and she described herself as feeling "fat, ugly, and stupid." Often Tom would reinforce this negative self-concept by pointing out her faults and describing her as "spacey" and "cute but slow" to his friends. Although he usually did this in a joking manner, Kathy nevertheless felt hurt by his frequent slights.

Tom, 36, held a master's degree in electrical engineering and worked for a large computer firm. In contrast to Kathy, he reported having great pride in his mathematical and analytical abilities and was quite vain about his physical appearance and his popularity. He spent five or six nights a week (as well as most of the weekend) exercising or meeting his friends at local nightspots, usually without Kathy. Kathy described Tom as extremely good-looking and very intelligent.

During the initial therapy sessions, both Tom and Kathy implicitly considered her to be the partner with a problem (what some therapists term "the identified patient"). As a result, both partners discussed their marital problems in terms of Kathy's irrational reactions to Tom's behavior. Tom often portrayed her as a jealous neurotic who continually suspected her innocent husband. For the most part, Kathy agreed with this interpretation of her behavior.

> **Therapist:** I'd like you to describe what goes on when you argue. Perhaps a concrete example would make it clear.
>
> **Tom:** It happens all the time when I look at other women. Take Saturday night for example. Remember? The girl in the sports car?
>
> **Kathy:** Oh, yeah.
>
> **Tom:** I knew that if I even glanced, I'd never hear the end of it.
>
> **Kathy:** Well, you see he's got this fetish about Oriental girls; I think he has ever since Vietnam. (Tom rolls his

eyes, obviously restraining a comment.) And it's like I can't compete with them because I'm not one. It's kind of hard for me to deal with when he looks at other women because I always have to wonder. I guess that's a typical jealousy reaction, but I think that's my major problem: I know I can't compete with what he's always looking at.

Therapist: You seem very worried about competing. What's at stake?

Kathy: Losing him. I guess that's what's at stake. Or his attention not focusing on me; instead it's on someone else.

Tom: Well, come on. My attention can't be on her 24 hours a day, can it?

At the third session, Tom voiced his frustration at not being able to correct what he considered to be "Kathy's problem." He complained of feeling depressed after each session, saying he felt so bad that he couldn't have fun when he went out. He decided to discontinue therapy. Kathy felt that therapy was helping her and pleaded with Tom to let her stay. Tom agreed that therapy would "be good for her" and agreed to allow Kathy to continue with individual therapy.

The initial stages of individual therapy with Kathy focused on the different expectations she and Tom had of each other and the different roles each of them enacted in their relationship. As these issues were discussed, Kathy's almost total dependence on her husband and his opinions became clear.

Therapist: So, you're saying that you both want different things, is that right?

Kathy: What Tom was saying is that he doesn't solely need me to be happy. He says that the only way I'll be happy is to spend 24 hours a day with him—and that's basically true.

Therapist: Is it?

Kathy: Yeah. I mean, I would give up everything just to spend time with him. Like if I had the day off, I'd putter around the house and the yard and then meet him for lunch. Now if *he* had the day off, he

> wouldn't bother to meet me. He'd go off on his own and have a great time.

Therapist: And that's the problem.

Kathy: Right.

☐ PERSONAL HISTORY

Kathy described her family as tightly knit and "typically Polish." When asked to elaborate on this term, she stated that her family is very close and has traditional, conservative values. Kathy described her father as having a strong, dominant role as the head of the family. Her mother fulfills a nurturing role; she takes care of the domestic needs of the family (i.e., the housekeeping, food preparation, laundry, etc.) and works as a secretary for her husband. Her father's income also supports both of Kathy's grandmothers.

Kathy described her own role in her family as that of a good, obedient daughter. Throughout her life she had always looked to her parents for advice and had rarely made a decision independently, even as late as college. Her parents were also very strict with her throughout her college years. Kathy described several instances of her parents' control in the course of therapy; she seemed particularly resentful of their meddling during her college years. Kathy's parents chose her college for her. They imposed a midnight curfew on her when she was home on vacations, and they also imposed a curfew on her when she was at school. Kathy recalled the time when she was a junior at college and her parents wouldn't allow her to attend any sorority parties because they would "keep her out too late."

Kathy appeared to maintain this role after college. For example, during therapy she revealed that she began to develop ambivalent feelings about Tom in the months before their wedding. When the therapist asked why she decided to get married anyway, she responded that her parents had gone to a lot of trouble planning the wedding and that she didn't want to disappoint them.

Kathy described herself as being very submissive in her marriage as well. Her nights were very lonely because she spent most of her evenings alone watching television and waiting up for Tom. Although she hated being alone, she felt that going out with friends "just wouldn't be right." Sometimes Tom would call and invite her to join him and his friends at a bar. When she arrived, she would often find him drunk and flirting with another woman.

On several occasions in the past year, she had had to drive him home from a female co-worker's apartment. Tom did not deny these occurrences, but he stated that they were "nothing serious." Kathy felt both furious at Tom's insensitive attitude and foolish about her own willingness to put up with it. As a result of this sort of behavior, Kathy has become increasingly ambivalent about remaining in her marriage. Much to her surprise, her parents (who had always rejected the notion of divorce) suggested recently that she seek a legal separation from Tom. This suggestion has served to intensify her ambivalent feelings. On the one hand it compelled Kathy to defend Tom (and implicitly herself), but on the other hand it also made her look at her life with a more critical eye.

☐ CONCEPTUALIZATION AND TREATMENT

Kathy has a long history of defining her identity in terms of important other people in her life, first her parents and now her husband. She has always obeyed her parents' relatively strict rules for her behavior, even when she was hundreds of miles away from them at school. To varying degrees, her college, her husband, and her present home have all been decided for her. On a more subjective level, Kathy frequently accepts her husband's critical views of her appearance and intelligence, despite objective evidence to the contrary. In short, her extreme dependence on the opinions of her husband and her parents, her persistent tendency to consider others' needs and wishes as more important—or at least more justified—than her own, and her inability to make an independent decision or to form an identity independent of those close to her clearly indicate a Dependent Personality Disorder.

According to her therapist, Kathy's dependent characteristics in all likelihood are the result of her adoption of a submissive, nurturant role from early in her life. Great pressure has been put on Kathy to assume this role, first by her traditional parents and later by her insensitive husband. Moreover, our society has a long history of emphasizing the importance of a woman's passive and nurturant characteristics while de-emphasizing the value of a woman's independence and intellectual abilities. It is not surprising, then, to learn that Kathy's boss routinely assigned mundane tasks to her and her female co-workers while he entrusted projects entailing greater responsibility to male employees, even those with much less experience. Although biases of this type have become less obvious over the past few decades, they nonetheless pervade many areas of our culture, and physically attractive women such as Kathy have been especially prone to this type of bias. It is possible that these subtle (and in some cases blatant) forces have induced her to channel her energies away from a career in biology and to focus them instead on modeling and aerobics, perhaps because these are activities that our society considers more appropriate for attractive women.

A clear instance of this influence occurred when Kathy and Tom discussed the possibility of her changing jobs. When Kathy described how frustrated she was with her position at the water commission, Tom suggested that she quit and become a waitress at a bar he frequents. He said that she could meet many new people and that the tip money was good. At first she became despondent at the thought of becoming a waitress and constantly having to deal with strange men who were often drunk and verbally abusive. In spite of her reservations, though, Kathy seriously considered Tom's suggestion. Finally she rejected the idea because it would mean that she would have to work late and thus would see her husband even less than she does now. Her decision was ultimately based on what would be good for her relationship with her husband, not what would be good for her.

As this example shows, Kathy was rarely encouraged to develop her own abilities, rather she was reinforced for conforming to other people's wishes and expectations. Perhaps as a result of this lifelong attempt to adopt roles that others have mapped out for her, Kathy has developed a rather superficial self-concept based on her submissive nature and her physical attractiveness. The following incident illustrates how important her appearance (or more accurately, her husband's opinion of her appearance) was to her self-image.

> **Therapist:** You say that you're fat. Tell me, why do you consider yourself overweight? You look fine to me.
>
> **Kathy:** I could still lose a little in the hips. I used to be a lot thinner, you know. Last year, when I really started getting into aerobics, I pretty much stopped eating. I got down to 105 lbs. (Kathy is 5'8" tall.) I thought I still had a little ways to go, but Tom said I looked *too* thin. He said I looked skinny and not athletic. Boy, was I surprised at that! Anyway, I guess he was right because I started having stomach problems then, and my doctor told me that I was 25 pounds underweight. I don't know what sort of standards he (the doctor) uses, but I don't want to be that heavy. I try to stay around 115 for Tom.

Therapy for Kathy involved a two-stage process. First, the interpersonal and social pressures that were apparently determining her choices were identified. In particular, Kathy was made aware of the ways in which her husband and her parents attempted, perhaps unwittingly, to control her life. Second, Kathy was encouraged to explore her own wants, needs, and feelings and to accept them as valid. The goal of this stage of therapy was for Kathy to develop a more positive self-concept and a clearer sense of her own identity. It was hoped that this would enable her to become more self-aware and depend less on the approval of others.

Although Kathy recognized her frustration with her husband's behavior, at first she was unaware of the extent to which his attitudes affected her. For example, Kathy described how she would always check for Tom's approval whenever she got dressed. If his response to a particular outfit was negative (or even neutral), she would immediately change her clothes. If his response was positive, she would wear the outfit, even if she disliked it or felt uncomfortable wearing it. When Kathy was asked why she would wear something she really didn't like, she simply responded that she wouldn't feel comfortable with him if he thought she looked ugly or stupid. Such events were frustrating and demeaning for Kathy, and she resented having to do what Tom said; however, it never occurred to her that her opinions were just as valid as his.

Although Kathy became less dependent on the approval of others as therapy progressed, she continued to describe her life and her problems in terms of her husband and, to a lesser extent, her family. She also attempted to draw the therapist into a collusion where he would join Kathy in focusing on Tom's negative characteristics as the root of her troubles. Despite her increasingly negative attitude toward her husband, he remained a central figure in her life. Her sense of her own identity was still vague and unclear, and she had great difficulty describing her own feelings and needs independent of her husband's or her parents'.

Therapist: You said before that one of your goals is to be happy. Tell me, what do you think would make you truly happy? I guess what I mean to ask you is: What do you want out of life?

Kathy: Well, Tom thought it would be great if we both started enjoying doing what we each like to do. He thinks that if I could enjoy what I like to do more, then he could enjoy what he likes to do more, and we'd both probably be a lot happier.

Therapist: Um, that sounds like Tom's idea. What about you?

Kathy: Well, I don't know. I guess I try to be a good wife.

> You know, my parents always taught me traditional values, like being a good wife and having a good marriage. Those things were always really important to them. I guess that's what's expected of me.

Therapist: No, I don't mean what your parents thought. What about you? What do *you* want out of life?

Kathy: (pause) You know, I don't really know; I mean, I have absolutely no idea.

By reinforcing her for making independent judgments and sincerely seeking out her emotions, the therapist supported Kathy's attempts to explore her own thoughts and feelings without relying on the opinions of others. Initially Kathy was hesitant to put forth her own views and would often try to change the subject of discussion. But by carefully prodding her, the therapist encouraged her to accept her ideas and emotions as being valid and worthwhile.

Kathy: . . . and that's how it ended last night. (Her eyes begin to well up with tears.)

Therapist: What's making you sad now?

Kathy: (Openly sobbing) Look, you've really got me going now. I'm sorry about this.

Therapist: You don't need to apologize to me.

Kathy: (Wiping her eyes) Look at me. I bet my mascara looks really great, huh.

Therapist: Do you think that's important?

Kathy: No, I guess not.

Therapist: Now tell me, what's making you sad?

By the eighth session, Kathy had begun to develop a greater sense of her own autonomy. She began focusing less on the wants and needs of her husband and her family, and more on herself and her own expectations. However, she was still unconvinced as to the legitimacy of her own ideas.

Therapist: Tell me if I'm right. I've noticed a change since you started coming here, and that is that at first you came to try to change Tom, like "What could I do to make him act a certain way?'' Now it seems that your focus is on what you, yourself, could do. Do you see that or not?

Kathy: Yeah, because when I first came here, I really wanted us to work out, and I wanted us to stay together. But I'm not so sure anymore. It's like, well, maybe I'm the one who has to change and not him . . . But will I be happy doing that?

As Kathy continued in therapy, her feelings of autonomy and self-reliance increased. For example, during the tenth session Kathy mentioned that Tom had been offered a job in Miami and had decided to accept it (without asking her opinion). Since Tom's job started a month before Kathy's contract with the water commission expired, she had to decide between the hassle of quitting her position early or having a one-month separation from Tom. She decided that the separation offered her a good opportunity to test whether she should relocate with Tom or seek a legal separation. After they moved out of their house she sublet a friend's apartment in Tampa and lived there until her contract expired. During this time, after considering her occupational opportunities and her expectations of the success of her marriage, Kathy decided to move to Miami to join Tom. She moved when her contract with the water commission expired.

Kathy's changing professional ambitions provided a good illustration of her increasing independence and self-confidence. When he was offered the job in Miami, Tom again suggested that she take a job as a cocktail waitress. This time Kathy rejected the idea immediately. More important, she based this decision on what she wanted and what would benefit her. She felt that a waitress job was insulting to someone with a degree and work experience in biology. Instead, she applied for positions as a biologist in the Miami area. She also asked her agents at the modeling agency to try to set up modeling assignments for her in Miami. As a backup, she applied to three graduate programs in biology.

Therapy was concluded with Kathy's move to Miami. At the final session (the fourteenth), she reported that she felt she had benefited from therapy. In particular, she thought that she had developed a better sense of her own identity and that she had acquired a more positive self-image and greater self-confidence. These changes were all gradual, resulting (presumably) from her therapist's frequent attempts to get her to accept her own views and wants. Interestingly, she also reported a greater satisfaction in her marriage, saying that she had the impression of being ''less trapped and having more options." She said that Tom was increasingly attentive and considerate. For example, during the first weekend of their separation, Tom surprised Kathy by flying back to Tampa to be with her.

☐ PROGNOSIS

In summary, Kathy appears to have made a number of significant changes in her thoughts and feelings that would lead to a lasting change in her personality. She began to depend less on the opinions of her husband and her family. As her sense of autonomy developed, so did her feelings of self-confidence and self-worth. In addition, these changes appeared to have affected her husband's behavior toward her; her increasing independence seemed to have fostered an increase in his consideration and respect. In general, the prognosis for Kathy and her marriage with Tom are good.

However, the persistent nature typical of personality disorders would caution against an overly optimistic prognosis. It is likely that over time Tom's narcissistic characteristics (a grandiose sense of self-importance and a lack of regard for others) will reemerge. As his need for Kathy decreases, it is possible that she may find herself becoming increasingly dependent on his attention and approval. This is especially likely since she has relocated to an area where she must establish and develop a new social support network. Unlike before, though, Kathy has made concrete plans for the eventuality that she may need to separate from Tom. Thus it is likely that Kathy will be less tolerant of a poor marriage and more able to live independently. To a great extent, then, Kathy's prognosis depends on her ability to develop and maintain relationships (either with her husband or with new friends) that support her newly found sense of accomplishment and autonomy.

☐ DISCUSSION

DSM-III-R describes a personality disorder as a long-standing condition characterized by relatively inflexible and maladaptive personality traits that cause either significant impairment in occupational or social functioning or subjective distress. In particular, a person would be diagnosed as having a Dependent Personality Disorder if he or she (A) allows others to assume responsibilities for major areas of life (e.g., choice of job or home, etc.), (B) subordinates his or her own needs to those of others, and (C) lacks self-confidence.

As a class, personality disorders (or, as they are commonly called, character disorders) have been difficult to diagnose reliably. One problem is that it is often difficult to distinguish the various personality disorders from one another. Furthermore, the traits that characterize these disorders are rather loosely defined and leave a great deal of room for a therapist's idiosyncratic interpretation. In addition, clients frequently display traits that are characteristic of two or more different personality disorders, making it very difficult for therapists to agree on the appropriate diagnosis. A second problem is that personality disorders differ from nonpathological personality traits only in degree, and the criteria used to warrant a diagnosis of personality disorder are subjective and difficult to determine. For example, how severely must a client's work or social functioning be disrupted before he or she suffers "significant impairment" in these areas? Similarly, how much "subjective distress" constitutes a personality disorder? These questions are difficult to evaluate objectively.

The case of Kathy represents an atypical personality disorder in that her characteristic traits and behaviors seem to indicate a single personality disorder. Furthermore, her presenting complaints clearly indicate that she was suffering a great deal of subjective distress and that her social relationships, particularly her marriage, were significantly impaired. Thus when she began therapy, Kathy easily met the criteria for a diagnosis of Dependent Personality Disorder. She appeared to be unable to function independently, and she passively allowed others to decide where she would be educated and where she would live. In addition, her overly critical self-appraisals reflected her low self-esteem and lack of self-confidence.

The sociocultural perspective hypothesizes that many psychiatric disorders result from people's maladaptive responses to dysfunctional roles that others induce them to adopt. Over time, such a person becomes accustomed to these maladaptive roles and incorporates the deficiencies they induce into his or her negative self-concept. In other words, the person will often develop a particular psychiatric disorder as a result of his or her efforts to adapt (perhaps unwittingly) to detrimental social roles. Often the first step in treatment is simply to identify these social roles. As the sociocultural factors that perpetuate these roles are examined, the person tends to become less susceptible to them. While it is not possible to shield a client from all these factors, a recognition of the most prevelant ones (particularly those that can label a person as "disordered") can alert the client to his or her options and thereby reduce the negative consequences.

Kathy's therapy involved two stages. In the first, Kathy and her therapist worked together to identify and analyze the social pressures that may have induced her to adopt an overly dependent role. The relatively strict expectations of her traditional upbringing, the seemingly callous behavior of her husband, and society's role expectations for attractive women were all isolated as possible factors. Just as important as these, however, was Kathy's inability to take charge of her own life. Once these different pressures were identified, Kathy could be made more aware of exactly how they were leading her to depend on other people and what she could do about it. Of course, Kathy would be unable to counter these various social pressures unless she first developed a clear sense of her own goals and a desire to obtain them. The second stage of therapy, then, was primarily devoted to having Kathy recognize and accept her own thoughts and feelings as valid and worthwhile. As Kathy incorporated these positive ideas into her emerging sense of self, her feelings of autonomy and positive self-regard increased, and she felt more capable of insisting that her goals and needs be respected.

This second stage of therapy utilized many of the techniques developed by humanistic psychologists. These techniques include providing clients with unconditional positive regard, at least to the extent that they are encouraged to explore and accept their ideas and feelings as valid and worthwhile; offering clients empathic understanding and listening to them from their own perspective; and attempting to be genuine with them by establishing a close and sincere therapeutic relationship. As this case shows, the sociocultural and humanistic approaches are not necessarily exclusive. Here, aspects of both approaches were combined in an attempt to identify the ways in which others influence Kathy and the ways in which she can draw on her strengths to shape her own life.

MALE ERECTILE DISORDER

Eclectic Therapy

❑ PRESENTING COMPLAINT

Jim is a 29-year-old actor living in Santa Monica, California, a suburb of Los Angeles. He has a daily job as a salesman in an electronics store. He frequently auditions for various roles in television shows and commercials, and he has had what he describes as "bit parts" in two movies. On the whole, though, he characterizes his acting career as "struggling."

For the past few years, Jim has experienced intermittent sexual problems, and once in a while this will come up in conversations he has with other actors while waiting for different auditions. Last week a fellow actor he had known for some time recommended that he see a therapist for his problems and provided him with the name of a therapist he had seen.

At his first session, Jim appeared to be somewhat hesitant and awkward. He looked off in the distance when he described himself, and he occasionally stammered and giggled nervously. After several minutes, though, he became a little more relaxed and described the precise nature of his sexual problems.

For the past three or four years, Jim has suffered from what he terms "off-and-on impotence problems." Sometimes he would have trouble maintaining an erection during intercourse, and he estimated that he successfully achieved orgasm "only about half the time, maybe a little less." Often he would lose the erection on attempting penetration, thus being unable to complete intercourse. Occasionally he would fail to achieve an erection altogether. This inability to maintain (or occasionally attain) an erection seemed to be limited to intercourse; masturbation, performed either by himself or by his sexual partner, almost always resulted in orgasm.

Jim states that his sexual problem is compounded by what he perceives to be a strong emphasis in the culture on black masculinity and sexual prowess. He says that the women he dates, both black and white, expect him to be a "terrific lover." In comparison to this relatively strict criterion, he feels that he does quite poorly, both in his own eyes and in the eyes of his partners. He says that they usually feel frustrated and hurt when he loses his erection. Most blame themselves and wonder if they are "not exciting enough" or if they "can't do it right." He added that one partner felt so upset that she locked herself in his bathroom and cried for several hours. Two or three of his partners have said that their evening with him was "a disappointment"; but most have not told him this directly. The problem has been a considerable source of anxiety for him over the past few years.

Jim is also concerned about the effects of this problem on his sexual relationships. Because of the embarrassment and anxiety he feels as a result of his disorder, he has often refrained from initiating sexual encounters for fear that he may not be able to "perform." Jim is convinced that his impotence problem is the primary cause of his inability to form lasting romantic relationships, and it leads him to feel anxious and depressed.

☐ PERSONAL HISTORY

Jim grew up in a blue-collar household in Los Angeles. He has two older brothers and a younger sister. His parents, neither of whom finished high school, held a number of different unskilled jobs while Jim was growing up. For the past 15 years his father has been employed by the U.S. Postal Service. His mother has worked as a waitress, a store clerk, and most recently as a beautician. His brothers both work "in the neighborhood"; his sister moved to San Jose after she was married. Jim could not think of anything unusual about his childhood. He summed it up by saying that his parents were "good people; they worked hard and always had food on the table."

Jim "barely finished" high school himself. For the past several years he has held various day jobs while auditioning for acting parts and taking an occasional acting class. Because of his unstable financial situation, he has lived with different people in various places in and around Los Angeles. Usually he would move in with someone out of economic necessity. Sometimes, though, he would move in with a woman he was dating—in some cases after dating for only a few weeks. He shares his present apartment in Santa Monica with a couple he met at a recent audition: a musician and his girlfriend.

Jim's sexual history is similarly unstable. He became sexually active at age 14 and describes his sex life in high school as "successful." He has had many female sexual partners since then; he estimates the number at "around five or six a year." For the most part he meets his sexual partners while auditioning for acting parts. He describes his partners as "people in the business" (actresses, script prompters, make-up and wardrobe personnel, etc.). He and his partners typically engage in sex very early in the relationship. Although he has had "numerous one-night stands," it is more usual for him to begin relationships with these women. (Sometimes, as already noted, he quickly moves in with this partner, usually as much for practical reasons as for romantic ones.) Typically Jim will date his partner for a few weeks or even a few months, but then the relationship will end abruptly. He estimates that the number of times the relationship is ended by him is about equal to the number of times it is ended by his partner. He is not presently in a steady relationship.

☐ CONCEPTUALIZATION AND TREATMENT

According to *DSM-III-R*, Male Erectile Disorder is a sexual dysfunction characterized by either (1) a persistent or recurrent failure to attain or maintain erection until the satisfactory completion of the sexual activity or (2) a persistent lack of subjective excitement or pleasure in the sexual activity. This diagnosis is not warranted if the dysfunction occurs only during the presence of some other disorder, such as a Major Depressive Episode. In addition, *DSM-III-R* asks clinicians to specify whether the disorder is the result of psychological causes (psychogenic), physiological causes (biogenic), or both; whether the disorder has been lifelong or was acquired after a period of normal sexual functioning; and whether the disorder is generalized to all situations or is situational in nature.

Jim's primary complaint is that he loses his erection, and in some cases his sexual interest, during intercourse. This has been a cause of anxiety and frustration for him and his sexual partners. His complaints seem to match the criteria for Male Erectile Disorder very well. Clearly his dysfunction was acquired, since he has been having sex for fifteen years and his symptoms began only a few years ago. His problem appears to be situational, that is, specific to intercourse. Since Jim is able to complete the sexual act approximately half the time and is able to masturbate to ejaculation, it is very unlikely that his disorder is biogenic.

Thus Jim's Axis I diagnosis would be of an acquired, psychogenic Male Erectile Disorder that is specific to situations involving intercourse. This diagnosis addresses only the objective manifestations of Jim's disorder. And Jim himself seems to focus only on this superficial level. However, several aspects of his complaints suggest that the picture may be more complex. The underlying cause of his dysfunction—his real problem—seems to be that he is a disorganized, impulsive, and anxious young man who lacks self-understanding and self-discipline. These characteristics would negatively affect both his sexual performance and his sexual relationships. On a performance level, self-discipline and self-confidence are needed to carry through the sexual act, especially to the point where the partner is satisfied. Lacking this, subtle signs of a performance deficit may erode the person's sexual behavior. On an interpersonal level, a certain amount of steadfastness and trust is required to work through the problems that inevitably crop up in relationships. It is also important to develop an awareness of other people's wants and needs.

Jim appears to be a good candidate for therapy. He is young and open in his descriptions of his actions and his feelings. Although he describes his problem almost completely in behavioral terms, he is nevertheless responsive to the suggestions and psychodynamic interpretations of the therapist. Finally, he is not resistant to the behavioral exercises, many of which involve masturbation.

The overall goal of Jim's therapy is for the therapist to act as an objective facilitator, a separate, "objective" person who can act to "spark" or regenerate his sexual behavior. Her eclectic background would be useful in providing Jim with a foundation of explicit behavioral training combined with dynamic analysis. As this implies, the therapeutic plan for Jim operated at two levels. On a cognitive and behavioral level, Jim received information about his anatomical functioning and his disorder. He also was given different practical exercises to increase his control over his sexual performance. These exercises are described below. On an emotional level, the therapist treated Jim through psychoanalysis. This analysis was aimed at increasing his psychological awareness of himself and others and at putting him back in touch with the parts of his personality that were repressed.

Since Jim initially sought a rather short, limited treatment for his sexual problems, therapy at first involved specific behavioral techniques and recommendations. Jim was taught the basic physiology of human sexual behavior, including a brief discussion of the four phases of the sexual response cycle (desire, excitement, orgasm, resolution). The primary value of this education was to eliminate any myths Jim may have had. For example, many males, unaware that they are physiologically incapable of attaining an erection during the resolution phase, complain that they are "impotent" after having sex. Simply informing them of the physiology of the male sexual cycle will often eliminate these anxieties.

Next, Jim was taught two specific techniques to improve his control over his erection (and thereby improve his confidence in his sexual performance). Instructions for these techniques were given during early therapy sessions; he practiced these exercises at home.

The first of these is Seeman's exercise, also called "The Start and Stop Technique." First, the patient is to masturbate to orgasm quickly to reduce tension about achieving orgasm. The next time he masturbates, however, he is to build up an erection gradually and try to maintain it before ejaculating. Eventually the patient should be able to attain an erection, maintain it for at least three to five minutes, let the erection slowly subside, and then be able to repeat the excitement, maintenance, and relaxation stages several times before finally reaching orgasm. The goals of this exercise are fourfold: (1) to develop control in attaining and maintaining an erection, (2) to increase the quality (i.e., the tumescence and the duration) of the erection, (3) to gain control over the timing of orgasm, and (4) to increase the patient's confidence in his sexual capabilities.

The second technique is known as the Kegel exercise. In this exercise the patient repeatedly tightens and loosens the pubococcygeal muscle (the muscle in the pelvis that restricts the flow of urine, sometimes called the "love muscle"). The patient is taught to flex this muscle in two ways: by tightening and relaxing it for long durations, and by rapidly flexing it for many repetitions. There are three general goals to this technique: (1) to increase muscle tone, (2) to stimulate the genital region, and (3) to increase the engorgement of blood into erectile tissue.

In addition to these physical exercises, Jim was also given some specific instructions pertaining to his sexual activity. Most important, he was told to restrict the frequency of penetration in order to save his strength and make those occasions more exciting. In the therapist's words, "Intercourse is exhausting. You may want to think of other ways to have sex with your partner and save intercourse for the weekends." The therapist's second piece of advice was to delay penetration until both partners were ready. Often penetration will fail simply because the penis has not been sufficiently stimulated. Similarly, intercourse may be painful or uncomfortable if the female is insufficiently aroused. Intercourse is more pleasurable for both partners after sufficient foreplay.

Jim was very responsive to these suggestions. He came to therapy regularly and reported that he performed the exercises as instructed. As therapy progressed, the focus of the sessions gradually widened from his specific sexual problems to more introspective topics. A particularly important topic of discussion revolved around Jim's perceptions of the expectations of his partners. He stated that most of his partners seemed to focus almost exclusively on orgasm and that he felt a strong pressure to perform. He also complained that the majority of his sexual partners lacked any deep emotional involvement, which decreased the quality of his sexual relationships with them. In general, he felt that sex was too "rushed and selfish." He thought that perhaps the stereotype of black men as being uncaring and macho was the cause for many of these problems.

The therapist responded that, if anything, these strong demands for performance and this uncaring attitude seemed to characterize the entertainment industry rather than the black culture. In actuality, Jim's complaints seemed to reveal more about himself than about these groups. For example, if Jim had a strong need for intimacy, why did he choose to earn his living (or at least to meet sexual partners) in an industry where so many people are considered shallow and selfish?

The therapist then widened the focus of Jim's therapy to deal with issues that did not relate directly to sex. Jim and the therapist discussed his feelings about his acting career, his anxieties about his chances of forming satisfying romantic relationships, and his need for intimacy, among other things. Gradually she raised issues that she felt were particularly significant for him, such as his disorganized nature, his impulsiveness, and his anxieties over becoming intimate with women. They discussed the importance of these characteristics for his sexual behavior and for his life in general. As he gained a better understanding of himself and his shortcomings, he slowly began to understand that he had walled off many aspects of his personality that he now wanted to recapture. For example, it was possible that his impulsive and nomadic living habits were manifestations of his refusal to acknowledge his need for intimacy and commitment, perhaps because of a deep anxiety that he would be let down. As he tackled these important issues, he very gradually uncovered these repressed parts of his personality. As he became more emotionally mature, he developed a better sense of what was missing in his life and how that affected him. Acknowledging these underlying needs made him more confident in his relationships and more secure in his own worth.

Jim has been in therapy for slightly over three years, and he seems to have made significant behavioral and emotional progress. After about two months he no longer complained about his "impotence," and the behavioral aspects of his problem were for the most part solved. Jim's first dynamic breakthrough came after about six months of therapy. He told the therapist that he found himself being more choosy about his sexual partners. By limiting his relationships to those women whom he considered worthy, he greatly increased his chances of developing an intimate and lasting relationship. It seems that this process paid off; for the past fifteen months he has been in a steady relationship with the same partner. He has also made a great many other self-discoveries; in general, his emotional awareness of himself (and, for that matter, of his girlfriend) is at a much more sophisticated level than it was when the therapy began, and he is better able to assess his sexual and emotional needs. He also feels ready to commit to a long-standing, intimate relationship. It is likely that these self-discoveries will help prevent him from developing psychological problems (manifested through anxiety, depression, or sexual dysfunctions) in the future.

❑ PROGNOSIS

The prognosis for Jim is good. He quickly eliminated his sexual symptoms and has continued to find out about himself and grow emotionally. He has reduced many of his impulsive behaviors (e.g., moving in with a new lover after only a few weeks), and the level of anxiety about his career and his relationships has decreased. He has developed greater awareness of the needs of his sexual partner(s), and he appears to have the ability to maintain a more mature, intimate relationship. Jim is very satisfied with the gains he has made in therapy.

In general, a patient's prognosis in these sorts of cases is based on two factors: his or her responsiveness to therapy and his or her underlying emotional stability. To a large extent, those patients who are willing to listen to the therapist and to perform the behavioral exercises generally show noticeable behavioral improvement after only one or two sessions. When therapy does not prove to be effective, it is often because the patient is not in touch with his or her repressed feelings of depression and anxiety. Unless the patient is first willing to acknowledge these underlying issues, the chances for lasting behavioral changes are relatively low. In addition, patients who are less emotionally stable are generally less amenable to therapy, particularly that which involves a great deal of introspection and self-discovery.

❑ DISCUSSION

An initial consideration in conducting therapy for sexual dysfunctions is to establish clearly that the behavioral problems are psychogenic. One indication of a psychogenic dysfunction is a prior history of normal sexual performance. In Male Erectile Disorder, for example, males who were previously able to achieve erections and then lost this ability (a condition frequently termed "secondary impotence") most likely suffer from a psychogenic disorder. Those who have never achieved a satisfactory erection (a condition termed "primary impotence") most likely suffer from a biological condition. A more reliable indication of whether erectile dysfunction is psychogenic or biogenic is the Nocturnal Penile Tumescence Test, or NPT Test. All normal functioning males have erections during REM sleep. In the NPT Test, the circumferences of the base and tip of the patient's penis are measured while he sleeps. If the patient shows no sign of an erection during REM sleep, he most likely has a biogenic erectile dysfunction. If the patient does have erections, however, it is probable that his erectile dysfunction is psychogenic.

In the past, most therapies for sexual dysfunctions employed traditional psychodynamic analysis consisting of a series of interviews with the patient conducted in the therapist's office. Specific behavioral "exercises" were not used; in fact, the patient's specific sexual complaints were seen as merely a manifestation of underlying neuroses and were dealt with only tangentially. After the rise in popularity of behavioral sex therapists (e.g., Masters and Johnson; Kaplan), sexual dysfunctions began to be treated almost exclusively with direct behavioral techniques. Currently most sex clinics offer some sort of behavioral sex therapy, such as the Masters and Johnson Sensate Focus program.

An important aspect of these behavioral exercises is that they rely heavily on the cooperation of a support partner. For example, the Masters and Johnson Sensate Focus program has the partners take turns as they go through three steps of the exercise: caressing, genital stimulation, and nondemand intercourse. After the partners have become comfortable with each other and more interested in each other, the couple moves on to the next step. One shortcoming of this type of treatment is that an uncooperative or unsympathetic partner can hinder or completely obstruct the progress of both partners. Some patients lack a partner with the required emotional maturity to carry out the program; other patients lack any steady partner whatsoever—as was the case with Jim. For these reasons, behavioral exercises that require only the patient's participation are often the treatment of choice.

The eclectic therapy presented in this case combines behavioral treatments with psychodynamic therapy. Specific exercises are seen as very useful in surmounting the particular problems, especially during the early stages of therapy. Providing the patient with psychodynamic analysis is seen as crucial in bringing about lasting behavioral changes. Thus it is vital for an eclectic therapist to receive training in both the behavioral techniques and psychoanalysis. As Jim's therapist states, "The patient needs to derive benefit from both the behavioral and the emotional aspects of therapy, and I can only take him as far as I've come myself."

An aspect of this case that has so far not been discussed is the gender of the therapist. For the behavioral aspects of treatment, this issue is of little consequence. Once the patient's initial discomfort and awkwardness about discussing his problem is overcome, therapists of both genders seem to be equally capable of providing instructions for behavioral exercises. Where this issue becomes somewhat more important is in discussing the dynamic issues of the case. Therapists of both genders have their advantages. Male therapists may facilitate the transference relationship and may be seen as more knowledgeable about the problem. Female therapists, however, are generally seen as more approachable, less threatening, and better able to provide an idea of what will satisfy the patient's partner. Generally speaking, however, this difference is relatively minor; the therapist's qualifications, experience, and talents are considered to be more important factors than gender for successful therapy.

Like Jim, many patients seeking therapy for sexual dysfunctions expect a direct, short-term behavioral therapy. When therapy begins to focus on more dynamic issues, some become uncomfortable. These patients either quit or switch to a more purely behavioral approach. Others, though, believe they can make gains from analysis and stay in therapy long after their behavioral symptoms disappear.

Sexual disorders can affect anyone at any age; however, most sexual dysfunctions affect young people, usually in their 20s or 30s. The one exception to this trend is Male Erectile Disorder, which is more common in men in their 40s and 50s (although in this case Jim was only 29). Ironically, older men are generally more resistant to therapy. Perhaps because of their more traditional sexual upbringing, they are less willing to perform the different exercises, especially those involving masturbation. As a group, they also seem to be less self-aware and less amenable to self-discovery. It seems that one effect of the more permissive sexual attitudes in society, then, has been to make men more amenable to therapy.

Although the "new morality" has brought about more open attitudes toward sex and sexual therapy, it has also engendered some new problems. In the past, young people typically either had to wait until they could have sex legitimately (i.e., until they were married) or they had to limit their sex to furtive encounters. As sexual mores loosened, sex became more widely available and more widely accepted. Now, for the first time, many young people are complaining of feeling "bored" with sex and of lacking sexual desire. Second, negative sexual impulse behaviors, such as "date rape," are becoming more frequent. It is possible that some people construe sexual behavior as being appropriate and even expected. Third, many young people are unwilling to delay their desires for sexual gratification; instead they seek instant pleasure and enjoyment. As a result, many sexual relationships have the quality, as Jim noted, of being "rushed and selfish." As young people become more sophisticated about sex, it is likely that the nature of their complaints will shift. On the whole, the complaints being brought to sex therapists will most surely continue to reflect the changing sexual attitudes of society.

BIPOLAR DISORDER WITH MOOD-CONGRUENT PSYCHOTIC FEATURES

Eclectic Therapy

□ **PRESENTING COMPLAINT**

Julie is a 20-year-old sophomore at a small Midwestern college. For the last five days she has gone without any sleep whatsoever; she has spent this time in a heightened state of activity that she describes as "off the wall" and "out of control." For the most part, her behavior is characterized by strange and grandiose ideas that often take on a mystical or sexual tone. For example, recently she proclaimed to a group of friends that she did not menstruate because she was "of a third sex, a gender above the two human sexes." When they asked her what she meant, she explained that she is a "superwoman" who can avoid human sexuality and still give birth. That is, she is a woman who does not require sex to fulfill her place on Earth.

Some of Julie's bizarre ideation has taken on a political tone. One instance involved global disarmament. She felt that she had somehow "switched souls" with the senior senator from her state. From his thoughts and memories, she developed six theories of government that would allow her to save the world from nuclear destruction single-handedly. She went around campus explaining these six theories to friends and even to professors, and she began to campaign for an elected position in the government (even though no elections were scheduled at that time). Nevertheless, she felt that her recent experiences made her particularly well suited for a high position in the United States government, perhaps even President.

During this time, Julie was worried that she would forget some of her thoughts, and she began writing these thoughts everywhere: in her notebooks, on her personal computer, and even on the walls of her dormitory room. Julie's family and friends, who had always known her to be extremely tidy and organized, were shocked to find her room in total disarray, with hundreds of frantic and often incoherent messages all over. By and large these messages reflected her disorganized, grandiose thinking about spiritual and sexual themes.

By the end of the week, Julie was beginning to feel increasingly irritated and fatigued. She began having difficulty walking, claiming that her right leg was numb. At this point her dormitory resident assistant brought her to the college health service, and she was seen by the therapist on call.

Julie spoke very rapidly in a rambling, loose style. Finally, when her delusions (strange systems of thought based on false or bizarre foundations) were made clear to her, she realized that she was in need of help and did not resist the therapist's recommendation that she be hospitalized immediately.

> **Therapist:** Well, Julie, what brings you here?
>
> **Julie:** I have a lot of trouble walking and I need to walk because I have so many things to do before the election, like make up posters and TV spots and interviews and all that stuff.
>
> **Therapist:** What about your leg? What's wrong with it?
>
> **Julie:** Well, sometimes I can't feel it because it's really my boyfriend's leg and I can't always control it.
>
> **Therapist:** You just said that your leg is really your boyfriend's leg. Is that right?
>
> **Julie:** I did? Uh-oh. You know, this has happened to me before, the leg thing. I had a lot of strange thoughts then, too. I had to go to the hospital.
>
> **Therapist:** I think this may be the same sort of thing, and you may need to go to the hospital again, OK?.
>
> **Julie:** Allright.

Previous Episodes

In the course of subsequent therapy, Julie described two earlier episodes of wild and bizarre behavior. These episodes alternated with periods of intense depression.

Julie's first manic episode appeared during high school. In the summer between her junior and senior years, Julie went to a tennis summer camp where she developed a strong attraction toward one of the boys. She had never had these feelings before, and they frightened her. She became extremely self-conscious of her sexual thoughts, and she became convinced that her bunkmates were constantly watching her and were able to read her mind. Although she never developed a relationship with the boy, she felt that she could not stand to be so near to him; she had to leave the camp and return home. She felt "safe" at home, and her agitation quickly subsided. She did not date during the remainder of the summer or during her senior year, which passed with no further incidents.

At the end of the summer, Julie went off to a private university in the East. After being away at college for ten days, she developed a severe depression as a result of not coping with "being on her own." She could not bring herself to attend classes or any campus activities. She suffered from a number of somatic difficulties characteristic of depression, including poor appetite, insomnia, an inability to concentrate, and difficulty in locomotion. After two weeks Julie left school and was admitted to a psychiatric hospital near her parents' home. While in the hospital she was given antipsychotic medication, haloperidol, which is known by the trade name Haldol. She also attended psychodynamically oriented group and individual therapy. Gradually her depressed symptoms dissipated, and she was discharged after seven weeks.

At the beginning of the next school term, Julie enrolled in a private university in the Midwest. Her past anxious and depressed episodes made her feel as though she had missed many social opportunities commonly experienced by people her age, and she decided to make a change and have a "real college experience." Julie made friends with a group of students who smoked, drank, used recreational drugs, and engaged in casual sex. Over the next several weeks she became increasingly irritable and restless, and she had difficulty sleeping and concentrating. Her use of marijuana and cocaine steadily increased, as did her reckless behavior. Her most disturbing memory was of the morning when she awoke and found herself in the bed of a male student whom she didn't know.

After half a semester she entered her second, and most severe, manic episode. She developed clearly bizarre thoughts and behaviors that revolved around themes of responsibility, sexuality, and religion. First she noticed that she acquired several compulsive rituals. For example, she washed her hands whenever she thought about sex. She believed that everyone was watching her and knew about her experiences with drugs and sex. She was deathly afraid that someone would somehow "expose her." Paradoxically, she often felt as if she could control the world; at times she felt that she could prevent nuclear war, and at other times she felt personally responsible for nuclear explosions that she believed had occurred already. She also suffered from what she described as a "Jesus Christ Delirium." She felt a special empathy with Christ, and she had what she later believed to be auditory hallucinations of Christ talking directly to her. She wanted to "merge with the higher spirits," and at times she felt her body floating. Her delusions often included ideas about the special significance of parts of her body. For example, she felt that one side of her head was "sensitized" to receive thought messages from Christ. Many times she also attempted to include other people in these delusions. Once her boyfriend saw her pressing her legs together and caressing her breasts with her hand. When he teased her about how "sexy" she looked, she tried to convince him that her right leg and hand were actually his, and that she was really stroking his body.

As she gradually lost control over her psychotic behaviors, she began to get the attention of university officials. For instance, several students complained to her resident assistant after they witnessed her chanting "Work . . . Work . . . Work . . ." over and over while riding up and down in an elevator. One day during a lecture she was attending, she began babbling about finding the Holy Grail. At first she only muttered to herself, but eventually her incoherent babbling became audible to the entire class. She ran out of the classroom and wandered aimlessly around the campus. Finally she was hospitalized as a result of her gross delusions.

Julie was admitted to the university hospital, where she was put on antipsychotic medication and lithium. She was again enrolled in psychodynamically oriented group and individual therapy, where she developed a good relationship with her psychotherapist. After about a month of intensive group and individual therapy her bizarre ideation gradually diminished, and she was released and returned to school. Although she was told to continue taking lithium, she complained of the nausea and diarrhea it caused and soon discontinued taking it.

Approximately a month after leaving the hospital, Julie began to feel depressed. Again, she experienced difficulty with eating, sleeping, and concentrating. She discontinued her favorite pastime, painting, and stopped going to classes. Finally she withdrew from the university and returned home. She was not treated for her depression, which gradually lifted during the summer. At the insistence of her parents, Julie then enrolled in a small college near her Midwestern home.

☐ PERSONAL HISTORY

Julie grew up in a "traditional Catholic-Irish home," and she described her parents as overprotective and demanding. Of the five children, she was the one who always obeyed her parents and played the role of the good girl of the family, a role she describes as "being the Little Miss Perfect." Julie stated that she was quite dependent on her parents and that they treated her as if she were much younger. It seems that Julie also adopted this view; she states that she sees herself as much younger than her peers in college. In contrast, Julie describes her siblings as rebellious. Her older brother openly defied the Catholic church by becoming an atheist, and her older sister made it known to her parents that she was sexually active in high school. Julie also describes her two younger sisters as defiant, but to a lesser extent.

Julie describes her parents as exceptionally strict with respect to sexual matters; they never discussed issues related to sex except to make it clear that their children were to remain virgins until they were married. Throughout high school her mother forbade her to wear make-up. Julie describes her childhood as that of a tomboy who played with trucks, fished, and always wore pants. She detested wearing dresses because they somehow made her feel a lack of control. She remembers being shocked and frightened when she began menstruating; she was especially distressed at the loss of control this entailed. Julie did not date during high school, and until recently had not had a steady boyfriend in college.

Julie's family history shows evidence of mood disorders: Her maternal grandfather received electro-convulsive-therapy (ECT) for depression, and her father's aunt was diagnosed as depressed at menopause.

☐ CONCEPTUALIZATION AND TREATMENT

Julie suffers from episodes of highly bizarre manic behavior alternating with episodes of moderate to severe depression. This pattern is indicative of Bipolar Disorder. While some therapists might take her grandiose and bizarre delusions to be signs of a psychotic disorder, her history of alternating manic and depressed episodes, and the manner in which her psychotic symptoms seem to correspond to her disordered mood (i.e., the delusions that appear during her manic episodes are primarily grandiose or mystical) point toward a diagnosis of Bipolar Disorder with Mood-Congruent Psychotic Features or, as it is more commonly known, manic-depressive psychosis.

Eclectic therapy draws on the assumptions of many different theoretical approaches and makes use of a variety of therapeutic techniques. Aspects of the biomedical, psychodynamic, humanistic, and behavioral schools, among others, may be employed. Typically, eclectic therapists are trained in one of the prevailing theoretical approaches and later combine elements and techniques from different schools in ways that they feel provide the best explanation for the etiology of a particular case and the most effective treatment for that patient. By and large, eclectic therapists initially focus on their patients' presenting complaints and on ways to control these problems. Once these immediate issues are addressed, therapy can begin to explore possible underlying causes. Typically, a patient's personal history is investigated to help the patient delineate important events that may have shaped his or her life. Next, the ways in which these events may contribute to the patient's present problems are discussed in individual or group therapy (or both). Finally, the therapist and the patient discuss how these insights may help the patient's long-term functioning. Thus eclectic therapy attempts to provide patients with a pragmatic and flexible approach to their problems.

In Julie's case, the initial consideration of her therapist was to control, and in time eliminate, Julie's florid psychotic symptoms. To accomplish this, her initial treatment consisted of somatic therapy in a controlled environment. Once Julie's therapist became aware of Julie's history of past manic and depressed episodes, he decided to hospitalize Julie and prescribe a combination of antipsychotic medication (in this case haloperidol, since it had been shown to be effective before) and lithium carbonate. Lithium carbonate, usually referred to simply as "lithium," has been shown to be especially effective in reducing the wild mood swings of bipolar patients. Once the bizarre psychotic features abated Julie would gradually be taken off haloperidol. However, she must remain on lithium treatment indefinitely to prevent the reoccurrence of her wild mood swings. Research and clinical experience have shown that lithium must be maintained at a blood level of approximately .5 milliequivalents/liter to control the disorder optimally. For Julie, this amounts to a dose of 1,200 milligrams/day.

The next stage of Julie's therapy was to examine her past experiences to identify some potential causes of her disorder. It appeared that Julie's problems might stem, at least in part, from her overly protective and strict upbringing. In addition to having strict values, Julie described her father as being overbearing and demanding and her mother as having perfectionistic standards bordering on obsessive-compulsiveness. One interpretation of Julie's behavior is that over time Julie developed a series of compulsive defenses to help reduce the anxiety caused by her parents' high expectations. For example, in an attempt to attain her parents' high standards of sexual purity (a task made difficult by the more open sexual mores of society), Julie denied her own sexual urges and feelings. An unfortunate result of this strategy was that she developed a great confusion about her own sexuality and to some extent her gender identity. These themes have pervaded her psychotic delusions.

To fulfill her parents' other strict expectations, Julie has attempted to be the perfect daughter, or as she describes it, the "Little Miss Perfect." She has always been a very conscientious daughter. She received straight A's throughout school, she has very neat personal habits, and she has always been willing to take on duties and responsibilities. Her psychotic compulsions—the most striking of which was her chanting "Work . . . Work . . . Work" around campus—are further indications of this defense. Her grandiose delusions of being able to bring about world peace single-handedly are symbolic expressions of her need to fulfill her responsibilities.

The term "Little Miss Perfect" also implies a repression of the sexual component of Julie's subconscious; describing herself with this term is another of her compulsive defenses. Her attempts to deny her sexuality began early on with her "tomboy" stage. It is significant that wearing dresses made her feel a lack of control as a child. At age 13 she was understandably shocked and frightened when she began to menstruate, probably because it conflicted so directly with her desire to deny her emerging sexuality. In fact, her first manic episode, which appeared during her summer camp trip when she was in high school, apparently resulted from her first strong feelings of sexual attraction. Later, when she was away at college, she was determined to rebel against her parents' strict expectations. Unfortunately, her experiments with drugs and sex seemed to overwhelm her compulsive defenses, resulting in a severe episode of manic psychosis. The themes of her psychotic delusions clearly illustrate her ambivalent feelings toward her own sexuality. On the one hand, her delusions about being a "third gender" convey her continued attempts to deny her sexuality, especially the physical symbol of her sexuality, her menstruation. On the other hand, many of her other thoughts express some attempt to reconcile her sexual feelings with her strict upbringing. Most notable among these was her explanation to her friends that she was a "superwoman" who could fulfill traditional sex roles without having to degrade herself with sex.

In addition to her problems in coping with her sexuality, Julie's psychotic ideation about spiritual themes seems to reflect her anxiety over trying to meet the relatively strict demands of the Catholic church while at the same time coping with the social pressures of modern college life. For many patients it is not uncommon for psychotic manifestations to incorporate a spiritual component, particularly for people with traditional religious backgrounds.

Often patients have a difficult time accepting the fact that they have repressed conflicts over their beliefs. Many firmly hold on to their (often unreasonable) principles and ideals and fail to understand how their internal standards may have contributed to their problems. In contrast, Julie recognized that her parents were very strict and at some level realized that her values were not the same as theirs. What Julie had problems with was perceiving the difficulty she had in defying the expectations of her upbringing. In a sense, Julie underestimated how strongly she still held her parents' values. Only gradually did she understand the extent of her own ambivalent feelings and how they might have an impact on her therapy.

Once the patient's underlying issues have been identified, the next step of therapy is to adjust self-expectations in a way that reduces the patient's anxiety while making sure that these adjustments are not so sweeping that they overwhelm his or her neurotic defenses. In Julie's case, she could not cope with the neurotic conflicts created by her experimentation with drugs and sex. Still, Julie seemed to have a need to free herself of at least some of the strict constraints imposed by her parents and her faith. With this in mind, Julie's therapist had her engage in a "mini-rebellion." After her hospitalization, Julie had to decide whether to stay at home for a while or to return to school. She was encouraged to return to school as a way of developing a sense of separation from her parents. This she did. Julie was also told to think about the conflict between her wants and her duties and how she might resolve these problems. A question Julie was asked to keep in her mind was, "When is Little Miss Perfect right, and when is she wrong?"

The therapist also suggested concrete ways to diminish Julie's neurotic defenses. For instance, Julie was told to try to become less concerned about her grades and to "loosen up" socially. At first, Julie had difficulty with this prescription. While she was still in the hospital, she had her parents bring her books so she could study (even though it was clear that she would not finish the semester). After she was released from the hospital, she refused to date and went out only rarely. Her therapist frequently encouraged her to go out and enjoy life, to let herself be more relaxed. Only gradually did Julie's social activities increase. After about four months, Julie mentioned that she had a boyfriend. She was urged to continue seeing him, provided he understood her needs and was supportive of her. In fact, the therapist met with the boyfriend and Julie together so that he could better understand the nature of her needs.

In addition to individual therapy, the therapist also got Julie involved in a depression therapy group. Julie found the supportive atmosphere of the group "extremely helpful" in overcoming her shyness about telling people about her illness. Since Julie was the only bipolar in the group and had by far the most serious illness, the other members of the group treated her with respect and, in some cases, awe. Julie told her therapist that she felt good being able to help other people just by being open and friendly.

The focus of therapy then shifted to altering Julie's impressions of the demands of her parents and the church through a process of cognitive restructuring. For example, one issue involved Julie's perception of sex. In therapy, Julie frequently admonished herself for having sexual fantasies and for her past sexual behavior. Her therapist tried to convince her that sex was not evil and that having sexual thoughts, and even engaging in sexual behavior, did not mean that she would automatically be sent to hell. The therapist emphasized that sexual feelings are common to everyone, particularly young women Julie's age, and that having sexual feelings was not a cause for shame or fear. A second issue was Julie's dependence on her parents' approval. Julie often refrained from doing something she would have enjoyed for fear that her parents might disapprove. To counter these thoughts, Julie was told that her mother was old-fashioned and had different ideas about life that were more characteristic of her generation than of Julie's. It was probable that her mother could not fully understand Julie's feelings, and created standards that were impossible for Julie to meet. It was emphasized that Julie should not deny her mother's values; rather she should accept them for what they were: another person's ideas, which were different from her own.

The final stage of Julie's therapy involved support and maintenance. Julie's weekly visits now dealt primarily with supporting her sense of autonomy from her parents, especially in the areas in which they disagreed. Just as important as her psychological support, these visits helped her maintain a proper level of lithium in her system. Once a month she had the lithium level of her blood analyzed to ensure that she maintained an effective yet safe lithium blood level.

☐ PROGNOSIS

As is the case with the majority of patients with Bipolar Disorder, Julie responded well to lithium treatment. At the present time (13 months after her most recent manic episode), Julie appears to be doing well. She is still in supportive therapy, which has now been reduced to a biweekly basis. She is still somewhat tense and anxious, but she has had no psychotic symptoms since her last episode. Julie is very bright (so far she has earned a 3.9 GPA in college in spite of her disorder) and has a great deal of insight into the causes of her problems. She describes her boyfriend as supportive and undemanding, and her relationship with him seems to be going well. Julie describes their sexual behavior as "a lot of necking and heavy petting"; they have not engaged in intercourse. Although Julie wants to keep sex "at bay" for the time being, she has begun to think about her future plans with her boyfriend and the possibility of getting married. Her main concern does not seem to be with her moral standards but rather with the possibility of a future pregnancy. Since lithium is contraindicated for pregnant women, she will need to interrupt her lithium therapy if and when she decides to become pregnant. She fears that she may relapse into another manic episode when she interrupts her therapy. This is a legitimate concern, but at the same time it shows how far Julie has come in coming to terms with her own sexuality and reconciling her underlying gender confusion.

In general, the severity of the psychotic symptoms Julie manifested would lead one to be cautious about her long-term prognosis. However, Julie's rapid response to lithium, her complete lack of residual psychotic features between episodes, and her keen insight into the causes of her disorder all argue against a diagnosis of an underlying psychotic pathology. Thus the prognosis for Julie seems quite good, provided she continues her lithium treatments and remains in a supportive relationship.

☐ DISCUSSION

Julie's presenting symptoms easily meet the *DSM-III-R* criteria for Bipolar Disorder, Manic Episode. For several weeks she had experienced an expansive and irritable mood. Her behavior had been characterized by physical restlessness, increased talkativeness, highly inflated self-esteem, a complete lack of sleep, profound distractibility, and an excessive involvement in activities that resulted in negative consequences (most notably her impromptu campaign for public office). In addition to these manic signs, her behavior included a number of clearly psychotic features, including delusions, hallucinations, and compulsive rituals. For the most part, the content of these psychotic features was clearly consistent with her inflated self-esteem (often involving her view of herself as having a unique relationship with supernatural powers). Thus the additional classification of Mood-Congruent Psychotic Features is warranted.

In the past, psychotic symptoms such as Julie's would commonly lead a therapist to form a diagnosis of Schizophrenia (Disorganized or Paranoid Type), Delusional (Paranoid) Disorder, or Schizoaffective Disorder. These diagnoses are difficult to differentiate, particularly during a patient's initial episode or when a patient's psychiatric history is for some reason unavailable. However, many of the characteristics of Julie's psychotic behaviors would exclude a diagnosis of a schizophrenic disorder under the *DSM-III-R* guidelines. First, her psychotic thoughts and behaviors are consistent with her mood, suggesting that they are in fact secondary to her mood disorder. Second, Julie appears to be completely free of any residual psychotic symptoms (e.g., social withdrawal, delusional thinking, etc.) when she is not in a manic episode. Third, Julie's history of past manic and depressive epsiodes, and her family history involving mood disorders, would support a diagnosis of a mood disorder over a psychotic disorder. In fact, the number of diagnoses of Bipolar Disorder has increased dramatically in the past few decades. At the present time it is unclear whether this increase is a result of more well-defined criteria, or whether it reflects an actual increase in the prevalence of the disorder.

The eclectic therapy that Julie received conceptualized her disorder as resulting from two primary factors: (1) a physiological, perhaps genetic, predisposition to develop a mood disorder, and (2) a complete breakdown of her neurotic compulsive defenses. As is typical with the eclectic approach, the therapist utilized therapeutic techniques from a variety of theoretical schools. Somatic therapy was recognized as instrumental in controlling her episodic mood swings and, consequently, her overt psychotic symptoms. Through a limited transference, the therapist attempted to gain a better understanding of Julie's conception of her parents and their demands on her. The term "transference" refers to having Julie emotionally react to her therapist as if he were a parent. The transference was limited in that it probed global expectations and feelings, not specific reactions to specific historical situations. Julie was also given concrete suggestions to modify her compulsive behavior. For example, she was reinforced (typically through the approval of her therapist and, later, her boyfriend) for increasing her social activities and decreasing her extreme attention to her academic performance. Julie only gradually and grudgingly began to follow this advice. She was taught to restructure her beliefs about her thoughts and feelings vis-à-vis those of her parents. Finally, she was given supportive therapy in an attempt to bolster her feelings of self-worth. Eclectic therapists do not see these different techniques as necessarily exclusive; instead they see the unique value of eclectic therapy as an approach that can combine different therapeutic elements into a comprehensive treatment plan.

Finally, some words of caution are in order. First, although the majority of bipolar patients tend to respond very well to lithium treatment, this treatment is not effective in all cases. Furthermore, lithium carbonate is a strong psychoactive agent that has many potentially serious side effects. Gastrointestinal difficulties such as nausea and diarrhea are common. Worse, prolonged elevated levels of lithium can result in irreversible kidney or thyroid damage. For these reasons, lithium treatment must be closely regulated. A second caveat is that it is common for patients with mood disorders to resist initial attempts at therapy. This resistance is usually explained dynamically as a loss of self-esteem following identification as a "tarnished" person. Thus psychiatric professionals, family members, and friends should make a special effort to provide the patient with a supportive atmosphere and gently persist in encouraging such a person to seek appropriate help.

DYSTHYMIC DISORDER, PRIMARY TYPE

Psychodynamic Therapy

❑ PRESENTING COMPLAINT

Mary is an attractive 23-year-old MBA student at the business school of a large Midwestern university. For years she has been frustrated and dissatisfied with her life. She has always done well academically, but lately she has noticed that she has little interest in doing her schoolwork and little confidence that she can do it well. With a degree of cynicism, she states that she has "big plans"; but she adds that she is constantly worried that she won't "cut it." She also fears that she will never be satisfied with life, even if she does succeed. She frequently feels irritable, despondent, and helpless, saying, "It's as if my entire life has been laid out for me. I don't feel like I have any choice about what I do. Worst of all, I think that it may all be a total waste." Lately her persistent negative cognitions have interfered with her ability to complete her teaching assignments and her thesis. She is easily distracted from her work and usually puts off doing it until weeks after it is due. She says that sometimes she hesitates because she fears that her adviser will reject the work as substandard (although this has never actually happened), and sometimes she puts it off because she doesn't "really care about it anymore."

In addition to problems with her academic work, Mary describes herself as having trouble establishing relationships with men. She describes a long-standing habit of picking up men (either at bars or at parties on campus) and quickly pressuring them to have sex with her. Within a week she then dumps them without an explanation, understandably engendering a good deal of hostility. Mary describes a recent example. Several weeks ago she met a man in one of her classes and asked him to come over for dinner. They slept together that night, despite his initial objections to having sex so soon. Two days later they saw a movie. When his reactions to the movie differed from hers, she stopped seeing him, telling him that he was uninteresting and that a relationship with him would be "a pointless waste."

Mary has also noticed that she "began drinking a lot" during the past year. She would drink heavily at campus parties or at bars, usually alone or with someone she was trying to pick up. She has also found that her drinking often makes her pass out after sex or after "cruising" the local bars. She complains that her drinking is also interfering with her academic work by making her tired and easily distractible.

Mary complained about her problems to a fellow student, who recommended a therapist he knew. At first she was resistant to being in therapy, but she eventually came to the conclusion that it might be a good idea. After an initial interview, the therapist decided that Mary should be seen for psychodynamic therapy three times a week. Mary agreed.

☐ PERSONAL HISTORY

Mary is the oldest child of four. Her father is a dermatologist; her mother has a bachelor's degree in advertising, but she did not pursue a career after graduation. Both grandfathers died young, and Mary's parents grew up in single-family homes. Mary's overall impression of her parents is that they were generally attentive and supportive, although paradoxically they seemed somewhat neglectful of her true needs. For example, initially Mary had difficulty learning to read. Her parents pushed her to try harder, but still her progress was very slow. It was not until after several months that her need for corrective eyeglasses was finally noticed.

After medical school, Mary's father did his residency in Chicago, where both parents' families were located. However, her father always had wanted to live in a rural area, so after his residency the family moved to a small town in Colorado. The consequences of this move were very important for everyone. Mary, who had become a voracious reader after she got her glasses, felt very unpopular in this small town, mostly because education and intelligence were not valued. After high school she applied to her father's alma mater but was rejected, partly, she believes, because of her poor education. She grudgingly settled for the local state university, which she felt was far below her intellectual capabilities. She described herself as "a big fish in a tiny pond."

Mary described her first two years of college as unremarkable. She spent her junior year of college in Europe, where she began a pattern of sleeping with men and then quickly breaking up with them. This pattern has persisted for the past three and a half years. When her therapist asked her how she felt about her relationships, Mary stated that she felt she needed to sleep with men in order to feel accepted and liked by them. After only a week or so, however, she would begin to feel bored with her boyfriend and would look for someone new.

After college Mary took a job in Chicago. After gaining a year of experience, she applied to several MBA programs. She was bitterly disappointed when her first two choices turned her down, especially since she had worked so hard to be a good candidate. At this time she began worrying about whether she would ever be successful. In particular, she complained about having to miss out on the best schools and the most interesting cities, saying, "I could never get anywhere that really mattered."

☐ CONCEPTUALIZATION AND TREATMENT

When Mary entered therapy she had experienced a chronic depressed mood for the past several years. She complained of a lack of energy, low self-esteem, poor concentration, and persistent feelings of hopelessness. Although these depressed symptoms were chronic, they were never of the severity associated with a Major Depressive Episode. Furthermore, although Mary complained that her depression disrupted her schoolwork, she nevertheless appeared to have been completing her assignments adequately. This constellation of symptoms clearly indicated the existence of Dysthymic Disorder, a persistent, low-level depression. Many therapists informally refer to this disorder as a "depressive personality." Since Mary's symptoms began before age 21 and did not appear to be related to any preexisting, chronic, nonmood disorder, her dysthymia would be categorized as Early Onset, Primary Type. In addition to her Dysthymic Disorder, Mary's intense emotional reactions to relatively minor events, her seemingly superficial attitude toward men, and her self-centeredness indicated an underlying Histrionic Personality Disorder. Many therapists might take Mary's extreme degree of dependence on others, primarily her mother and later her therapist, as indications of an underlying Dependent Personality Disorder. However, in most aspects of her life Mary functioned quite independently, and the majority of her life decisions were entirely her own. Thus a diagnosis of an underlying Dependent Personality Disorder would appear to be unwarranted.

Since the underlying dynamics that contributed to Mary's persistent mood disorder could be identified only gradually as therapy progressed, the initial sessions were rather unstructured. Mary was quite expansive in her initial sessions. She talked quickly yet carefully about a number of different global topics, including her dissatisfaction with her life, her need to be accepted, and the chances that she would be successful. She tended to focus on the "big picture"—that is, she worried about being successful and being loved, but she did not seem to think about just how she could go about becoming a success or how she could develop more satisfying relationships. She also appeared to feel a strong need to tell someone about her life, and apparently she saw therapy as a perfect opportunity. Initially Mary's therapist felt flooded by material, and she described Mary's self-descriptions as being like "water released from a pent-up dam." The first goal of therapy was for Mary to slow down and focus on specific topics and memories. She was also urged to apply the intellectual skills she possessed to the tasks at hand and not to get lost in the "big picture."

In therapy, Mary first discussed a series of dreams she had been having for the past few months. These dreams involved fears of being attacked by wild animals (which she called "monsters"), a topic she had not thought about since she was a small girl. When Mary was 3 or 4, she developed a terrible fear of the animals around their rural home. She was terrified that wild monsters would crawl up the side of their house and enter her window, and she dreamed about such occurrences almost every night. She reported feeling constantly worried by these thoughts, even though she realized that the monsters could never really get in through her window.

The therapist suggested that these monsters might represent some person or force that Mary feared during her childhood. She and her therapist then began linking the animals with her father, a person who could potentially hurt her and also someone who could get in through the window, that is, gain an understanding of Mary's real fears.

The therapist also discussed the transference process with Mary. By the way Mary eagerly described her problems, it was obvious that she felt a strong need to tell her thoughts and feelings to someone who would trust and protect her, someone like a father. Perhaps Mary saw the therapist as "another kind of father (although the therapist was a woman)," one who could better understand her. By pouring out her feelings to the therapist, Mary was in effect talking to her "father" about her father. Mary agreed that her father had been distant for much of her life, and she thought that the therapist might have a valid point. At this point, Mary returned home for the summer break. Therapy resumed on her return to school approximately three months later.

When she returned, Mary reported that she had been fighting with her mother quite frequently over the summer. As a result of this constant arguing, she and her therapist discussed the possibility that her images of wild monsters represented hostility that was directed toward her mother, not her father. (In hindsight, the therapist now realized this was why her being a woman did not seem to impede the initial transference process.) This possibility came as somewhat of a surprise to both Mary and the therapist, especially since Mary's initial descriptions (or, as they are often called, her "first layer of presentation") of her mother were always very positive. She described her mother as a loving and devoted parent who always put her family before herself. Now she had quite a different picture of her—a "smart lady who got robbed of a good career because Dad had to live in the middle of nowhere." Analysis now focused on her mother's frustrations and bitterness at being stuck in a small town in Colorado, feelings that Mary did not understand as a child.

This revelation changed the therapist's initial conception of Mary's childhood. At first it was assumed that Mary had the standard oedipal constellation of a stern, threatening father and a nurturant but ultimately unavailable mother. Instead, it appeared that Mary's father was the parent who was actually nurturant and undemanding, whereas her mother was strict and constantly pushed her to achieve. Mary found the weakness of her father and the assertiveness of her mother to be inappropriate qualities; each possessed the characteristics usually found in the opposite gender. It was now clear that Mary organized her world around her parents' interpersonal characteristics instead of their gender, but this left her in quite a dilemma with respect to her psychosexual identification. On the one hand, she could be like her dominant, assertive mother. That is, she could identify with her female parent only by adopting what she felt were masculine characteristics. On the other hand, she could side with her passive, nurturant father. She found herself unconsciously attracted to each, but paradoxically she could not fit with either. Since she could not fully identify with either parent, her inner world remained in a constant state of flux.

This confusion was clearly illustrated in Mary's inexplicable interest in a minor news story about Great Britain's Prince Charles and Princess Diana. She became very involved in this story and frequently discussed Diana's role as the "power behind the throne." Several aspects of Mary's current behavior also reflected this issue of sexual ambiguity. In particular, her persistent pattern of sleeping with men and then breaking up with them seemed to indicate a strong need for affection and caring combined with an intense fear of becoming dominated.

This ambivalence also emerged in the therapeutic relationship. During the first year of therapy Mary gradually became more and more dependent on the therapist. When the therapist went on vacation for a week, Mary panicked because she would have to miss three sessions. As Mary discussed these feelings, she began to realize that maybe she was becoming too dependent on therapy. She felt as though she was "being controlled from behind the scenes by a powerful female." At the first session after her therapist returned from vacation, Mary suddenly announced that she was cutting therapy back to one session per week and refused to discuss the matter with her therapist. At the next session, she angrily stated that she was quitting and left after 20 minutes.

One month later Mary phoned the therapist and asked her if she could continue therapy. During the session Mary stated that she was sorry and scared. In the weeks after she left therapy, her recent boyfriend had broken up with her, complaining that she was trying to use him as a therapist. Realizing that she needed to work out the issue of her dependence on others, she wanted to continue therapy "starting from scratch."

Now, for the first time, the therapist had the impression that Mary was more deeply involved in the therapeutic process. Mary developed a "questioning attitude" in which she was willing to discuss an important issue and analyze it. A prime issue for Mary was her need to be close to other people. She felt that there were boundaries between herself and others, and that she needed to break these boundaries to feel close. She admitted that this need might be why she always pushed men to have sex with her so soon after she met them. She also talked about her dependence on therapy. She described a dream she had had in which the therapist was coaching her in an important race. During the middle of the race, the therapist stopped coaching her and told her to finish the race on her own. This dream frightened Mary, and she said she felt frightened at the extent to which she trusted and needed someone else. She said she felt upset at her dependence and that she wanted to quit therapy, but she had decided that she should stay.

Therapy now focused on Mary's childhood. Her first memory was of an incident when she was 3 years old. Her parents had bought a cat, and she had become quite attached to it. After a few months, Mary's father had the cat put to sleep, having attempted unsuccessfully to housebreak it. Mary was afraid that she, like the cat, would be killed or abandoned if she were sick or messy. For the next year or so she did everything she could think of to show her parents that she was strong and healthy; she remembers downplaying her sicknesses and hiding her dirty clothes. At the time Mary felt abandoned by her parents; her mother was now busy with the birth of her brother, and her father (who was a resident at the time) seemed more inclined to get rid of problems than to try to fix them. In the midst of describing these memories during a therapy session, Mary began crying and sobbing. She wailed, "My kitty died, and no one cares!" The therapist asked her why this episode made her so upset now, over twenty years later. Mary replied that she was afraid that the therapist would not be willing to "fix" her and would abandon her instead. Mary then became afraid that therapy would not work and that it would all be for nothing; she later said that she cried during her entire drive home from the session.

Another clear childhood memory Mary had was of an event that occurred when she was about 7 years old. She remembered needing to be around her mother constantly, and that she could not stand being away from her. Often her mother had to order her to play outside with her friends. Once she became so upset at this that she threw a tantrum and broke a picture window. One night a few days later her parents went out for the evening. Afraid that her mother would never return, Mary turned to the baby-sitter and asked her if *she* would be her mother. This shocked even her little brother (aged 4). Mary says that her mother always made her feel special. Her mother always expected great things of her, and she pushed her to do her best at all times. She felt that this made her relationship with her mother very special, and consequently she had a difficult time accepting even short-lived separations. Gradually Mary recognized that her parents really did love her and that they were not going to abandon her because of her weaknesses. In fact, they (especially the mother) pushed her to achieve because they had ambitions for her.

These insights did not occur quickly or easily. Mary and her therapist would grapple with certain issues for weeks or even months. First, important memories and themes from her life had to be identified. Next, the importance of these issues in terms of Mary's life had to be determined. Often, important issues involving the transference between Mary and her therapist had to be discussed and reconciled. All the while, other practical issues relating to therapy and current issues in Mary's life needed to be discussed.

Mary had been in therapy for almost three years when she was ready to graduate from her MBA program. At this time she applied for various jobs around the country, and she decided to accept a position as an investment manager for a medium-sized firm where her chances for advancement were good. This firm was located in a small town about 1,000 miles away. Although she initially found it difficult to leave therapy, she also felt that moving would give her a chance to gain some independence. After her move, Mary began to write her therapist a long letter every week. In her letters she discussed the issues she found to be important in her life, particularly her difficulties in forming a relationship and the need to get reassurance while she set herself up in her new position. After several months Mary realized that writing letters was not a particularly effective way of dealing with these issues, and she finally asked to be referred to a local therapist. Her therapist recommended a therapist in the area, and Mary has since begun to see him for one session a week.

❑ PROGNOSIS

Mary appears to be doing quite well. She has been at her present job for approximately two years. She has received an early promotion and is getting a good deal of exposure within the firm. She has maintained a therapeutic relationship with the male therapist, and the fact that she is able to remain committed to a long-term, nonsexual relationship with a man is encouraging. Mary also seems to be experiencing more adequate relationships with other men, and for the past year she has had a steady boyfriend. However, she still appears to have some problems in making emotional commitments. She admits to having frequent flirtatious experiences with men (she describes herself as "peeking over the edge but not jumping off"), but so far she has refrained from her earlier pattern of sexual promiscuity. In short, she reports feeling much more optimistic about her career and her social relationships than when she entered therapy. She also reports negative mood less frequently in everyday events. Furthermore, she seems to have developed a sense of autonomy and emotional maturity in her relationships, which makes it more likely that she will be able to maintain these improvements in the future.

❑ DISCUSSION

As is typical for most psychodynamic therapies, the symptoms involved in the presenting complaint are not dealt with directly but are taken as symbolic representations of long-standing underlying pathologies. The development of a transference relationship with the therapist is the primary tool employed to uncover these underlying problems and bring them into focus. As the patient achieves insight into these unconscious traumas, the neurotic defenses that guard against them will no longer be necessary and will begin to dissipate. In Mary's case, a transference relationship with the therapist in which Mary became extremely dependent uncovered two underlying dynamic issues: her difficulties in forming an identification with her mother and her early fears of abandonment. As she relived these traumas, Mary experienced a cathartic release, and gradually her ambivalent attitudes toward her career and toward men (the superficial manifestations of these unresolved issues) diminished.

Mary's therapist was concerned that perhaps therapy was being ended prematurely. Although Mary seemed to have made a good deal of progress during her three years in therapy, she still had some issues left to resolve, particularly those relating to her relationships with men. Whereas many therapists would have encouraged Mary to put off moving and "fight for therapy," her therapist felt instead that Mary's increasing sense of autonomy (itself a therapeutic goal) made it important for her to pursue her career goals. Although their work together was not finished (as evidenced by Mary's letters to the therapist), in the therapist's opinion Mary had made enough progress to move on with her life without jeopardizing the gains she had made in therapy.

Several aspects of this case were somewhat unusual. First, it is rare for a patient to become so intensely involved in the emotions of his or her childhood memories. In contrast, it is much more common for patients to split off their emotions from the content of their stories. While Mary's intense affect may have aided her in fully reexperiencing her childhood traumas, at the same time it may have interfered with her ability to analyze their meaning rationally and thus achieve insight.

A second unusual feature of this case was the great sensitivity with which Mary was able to articulate the extreme dependence she felt on her mother and on the therapist. Again it should be noted that these insights did not occur quickly; Mary's sensitivity to this issue was well hidden and surfaced only after approximately eighteen months of therapy.

Finally, although many dynamic therapies are seen through to completion, it is not uncommon for some patients to interrupt therapy at some point. As the transference process begins to uncover repressed conflicts, patients become very commited to their analysts as well as to the work of therapy. But at the same time, the therapeutic experience may make them quite angry and fearful. These mixed emotions may cause some to feel a great apprehension about stopping treatment whereas others may discontinue treatment for months, years, or even permanently. In contrast, Mary appeared to have a short "panic reaction" to the realization of her extreme emotional dependence on others, and her willingness to return to therapy indicates an awareness of her need to address this issue. On the whole, Mary was an unusually sensitive and motivated patient who was responsive to the psychodynamic approach to therapy and made significant gains as a result of it.

CHRONIC SCHIZOPHRENIA, RESIDUAL TYPE

Pharmacological Therapy

□ PRESENTING COMPLAINT

Jerry was detained by U.S. Army MPs when he attempted to walk through an American army checkpoint on the East German border, ignoring the commands of several border guards. In their report the border guards stated that Jerry had said "something about pursuing freedom and living off the land," but that for the most part what he had said was vague and incoherent. During his detention Jerry was interrogated by officers at the checkpoint. He was calm, even passive, but he seemed to be completely unaware of where he was and the situation he had gotten himself into. He appeared to be an American around 50 years old, but this could not be confirmed since he carried no passport, travel visa, or any other identifying papers. In addition, he did not tell the army interrogaters anything specific about who he was or where he was from, saying only his name and that he was from "different places over there." He reported having no present address in West Germany, no steady means of support, and no means of travel. Somewhat stupefied, the officers asked him just what he planned to do in East Germany. Jerry replied, "Oh, just wander around, here and there. Nothing much—just see stuff, you know?" Jerry was then admitted to the camp infirmary for

71

psychiatric observation, where he was first diagnosed as schizophrenic. He was then admitted to a U.S. Army hospital in Coburg, West Germany. There he responded well to an antipsychotic medication. He was amiable and cooperative on the ward, and he was now able to tell the hospital staff some details about his identity and background. Through army records, the hospital was able to contact Jerry's parents in Munich, about 140 miles to the south. After five weeks on the ward Jerry seemed to be under control, and he was discharged to the custody of his parents, who reported that this was the third time Jerry had "wandered off" since he had moved to Munich the previous year. Realizing they could not control him while living in Europe but reluctant to commit him to an institution, Jerry's parents sent him to live near an aunt in Salt Lake City.

Jerry's aunt rented a small studio apartment for him and set him up with a job at a local supermarket. On his third day at the market, he walked off the job during his shift. Jerry returned to his apartment and did not go outside for several weeks; his aunt then became responsible for doing his laundry and shopping for his groceries. On one occasion, at 2 o'clock in the morning, Jerry somehow became locked out of his apartment. He began yelling and banging on the door, and after about twenty minutes he finally broke it down and went inside. After this incident (and numerous other complaints of his odd behavior by neighbors), Jerry's landlord began proceedings to evict him. Jerry's aunt promised to keep a closer eye on him and convinced the landlord to hold off on the eviction. She then found him a part-time job as a church custodian. After two weeks of spotty attendance, though, Jerry again wandered off the job. This time, however, Jerry did not return to his apartment. After three days Jerry's aunt contacted the police and reported him missing.

Seven months later Jerry was arrested for vagrancy in a small town outside Bakersfield, California. In the meantime, Jerry's parents had returned from Europe to the Los Angeles area. The police contacted his parents, who then drove out to Bakersfield to be present at his court hearing. A psychiatric evaluation, conducted on the recommendation of the county district attorney, found Jerry to be incompetent to stand trial. With the consent of his parents, Jerry was committed to a psychiatric institution for treatment. He then entered a psychiatric ward in a Veteran's Administration hospital located in a suburb of Los Angeles.

☐ PERSONAL HISTORY

Jerry's descriptions of his past are for the most part extremely vague and lacking in content. He is unable to specify any dates, places, or events in his life. Occasionally he does provide some information, but most often this is inaccurate. For example, Jerry once reported to a hospital staff psychiatrist that he was an only child, when in fact he has an older brother. As a result, the hospital staff is forced to rely on other sources of information (e.g., his parents, his brother, and his aunt; various medical, school, and military records; etc.) for the bulk of Jerry's background data. Although these secondary sources can provide most of the basic information on the important events in Jerry's life, they cannot describe his perceptions of these events or his emotional reactions to them. Sadly, this subjective information is irretrievable.

Jerry is the younger son of two in an upper-middle-class family. His father is a successful executive for a German automobile manufacturer; his mother has never been employed outside the home. According to his family and the available records, his childhood was unremarkable. He seemed to have a happy childhood and got along well with his family. He received good grades throughout school (mostly A's and B+'s). His parents recall that he seemed to have a successful social life in high school; he dated often and participated in football and track. After high school he enrolled at a large state university to study mechanical engineering. It was in college that his odd behavior first appeared.

Jerry's grades for his freshman year were considerably below his usual performance, averaging in the low C range. His professors, his roommate, and his neighbors in the dormitory confirmed that he was not working up to his potential; they reported that he would frequently miss lectures and assignments. He seemed unconcerned about making friends or becoming active in campus activities, and his phone calls home became more infrequent as the year progressed. During his summer break he refused to work at a job set up by his father and spent most of his time either alone in his room or wandering aimlessly around the neighborhood. When he first returned home from college, Jerry's high school friends frequently came by to see him, but he seemed uninterested in them and made no effort to maintain their friendship. Although Jerry returned to college for the fall semester, it appears that he stayed in his dormitory room for most of the term. His academic work continued to deteriorate, and he wound up failing every course. In addition to his academic difficulties, Jerry was beginning to cause serious problems in his dormitory. His roommate complained that he would spend almost all his time in his room either sleeping or mumbling to himself. He did not do his laundry the entire semester, and he often went without bathing for stretches of up to ten days. After eight weeks his roommate demanded to be transferred to another room. Over the winter break, Jerry was informed that he would not be allowed to continue at the university because of his academic and social difficulties. After his expulsion he was no longer eligible for a student deferment from military service.

Four months after he left the university Jerry was drafted into the army. According to his evaluation during basic training, Jerry was found to be of above average intelligence. However, his records also show that he lacked motivation and paid poor attention to instructions. He was described as a recruit who understood orders and instructions but followed them without any particular concern over what they were or whether he would execute them properly. After completing basic training, Jerry was assigned to an ambulance unit in Vietnam. Jerry's combat record was similar to his record as a recruit. Although he did not resist his orders, he had to be constantly supervised to ensure that he actually carried them out. He was involved in combat on several occasions and once received superficial wounds to the legs. After his combat tour, Jerry was assigned to work in the motor pool of an army camp in northern Texas. His stay at this camp was unremarkable aside from the fact that he again was quite indifferent about his assignments and required constant supervision to carry them out. Finally he was discharged from the army after his two-year period of service was completed.

After his discharge Jerry got a job working at a fast-food restaurant near Wichita Falls, but he left this job after about a month. Two weeks later he was arrested for shoplifting in Norman, Oklahoma. Apparently Jerry had attempted to walk off with several items from a grocery store. In light of his veteran status and his clean record, however, the store owner decided to drop the charges. For the next several years little was heard of Jerry, and his own accounts of this time are not particularly informative. Finally Jerry was arrested for vagrancy and disorderly conduct in Omaha after he repeatedly harassed passers-by in a park with strange and incoherent remarks on the order of: "Where's the freedom land?" and "I want to hear freedom ring!"

During Jerry's tour of duty in Vietnam, his father was transferred to the corporate headquarters in Munich, West Germany. While in the army Jerry corresponded with his family only rarely, and they heard nothing from him for the next three years. Through Jerry's military records, the Omaha police managed to identify him and contact his parents in West Germany. At the insistence of his parents, the court agreed to release Jerry to their care, and they took him to live with them in Munich.

☐ CONCEPTUALIZATION AND TREATMENT

The term "schizophrenia" refers to a collection of diagnostic categories characterized by the presence of severe disturbances in thought, behavior, and interpersonal relationships. These disturbances may be manifested in a number of ways, as described below. In addition, schizophrenia is an episodic disorder characterized by three distinct phases. During the *prodro-mal phase*, schizophrenics will show a significant deterioration of their social and cognitive functioning from a premorbid level. They tend to withdraw increasingly from social situations, neglect their duties and hygiene, display strange thoughts and emotions, and lose energy or initiative. This deteriora-tion in functioning, called "decompensation," is usually the first sign to other people that a serious disorder is present. Behavior changes during the prodromal phase are usually subtle. Other people generally describe schizo-phrenics as "acting differently from their usual selves."

During the *active phase*, markedly psychotic behaviors will emerge. These include delusions (organized thought systems that, while coherent, are based on clearly false or bizarre ideas), hallucinations (vivid but illusory percep-tions, usually auditory), disorganized thought patterns, odd speech, gross incoherence, inappropriate or restricted emotional reactions, and severe abnormalities of motor movement. *DSM-III-R* categorizes schizophrenics into five subtypes based on the constellation of symptoms they exhibit during this active phase of their disorder. These subtypes are described below.

As the more florid psychotic behaviors of the active phase recede, schizophrenics enter a *residual phase*. The symptoms of this phase are very similar to those in the prodromal phase, with the exception that emotional blunting (lack of emotional reactivity) and a neglect of one's duties are particularly pronounced in the residual phase. Other signs that may linger from the active phase are illogical thinking and some relatively mild delusions and hallucinations. The majority of schizophrenics display some cycling of active symptoms and residual symptoms for the rest of their lives; a complete cessation of symptoms, known as *remission*, is relatively rare.

DSM-III-R distinguishes five subtypes of schizophrenia based on the particular pattern of symptoms that are exhibited during the active phase of the disorder. These five subtypes are labeled the Catatonic Type, Disorga-nized Type, Paranoid Type, Undifferentiated Type, and Residual Type.

Catatonic schizophrenics are characterized by severe disturbances in psychomotor behavior. Catatonics are frequently mute and unresponsive to the behavior of other people. They may assume rigid, passive, or otherwise bizarre postures. In some cases catatonics also show brief periods of wild, excited, and purposeless activity. One unifying quality of virtually all catatonics is that they are almost completely unresponsive to their environ-ment.

Disorganized schizophrenics are also characterized by strange, incoher-ent, and often silly behavior. However, their symptoms reflect gross distur-bances in their thought processes as opposed to their psychomotor processes.

Their speech tends to be characterized by loose associations (drifting from one topic to another unpredictably), neologisms (made-up words others do not understand), and clanging (silly, rhyming sounds). Disorganized schizophrenics also tend to show emotions that are utterly inappropriate for their current situation, such as crying on hearing a joke. In contrast to catatonics, most disorganized schizophrenics appear to be somewhat responsive to their enviroment. They will answer questions, notice objects, and recall events. To most people, however, these responses seem bizarre, incomprehensible, and unpredictable.

Paranoid schizophrenics are preoccupied with elaborate delusional systems, usually relating to themes of grandiosity, persecution, jealousy, or suspiciousness. The cast of these delusional systems typically involves divine or supernatural beings, important figures from the schizophrenic's life, or images from history or the media. Unless they are in the process of acting on their delusions, paranoid schizophrenics usually appear to act fairly normally, at least at a superficial level. As they become more involved in their strange ideation, however, the full extent of their delusional thinking becomes apparent to other people.

Undifferentiated schizophrenics either display prominent psychotic symptoms from more than one of the above categories or show symptoms that do not fit easily into any of the above categories. Thus Schizophrenia, Undifferentiated Type, is a "garbage can" label that characterizes schizophrenics who exhibit the psychotic symptoms of an active phase but cannot be described by any of the three known subtypes.

Schizophrenics categorized as Residual Type have not shown a clear history of the bizarre or delusional behavior of an active phase. However, they do exhibit relatively mild signs of schizophrenia such as disrupted daily functioning, social withdrawal, blunted affect, and illogical thinking. Most residual schizophrenics have a long-standing history of more or less continuous symptoms. In some cases there is evidence of a past active phase, but the details of this behavior are not sufficiently clear to allow a diagnosis of any particular subtype. Residual schizophrenics are responsive to specific stimuli in their environment, but their lives taken as a whole generally lack meaning and coherence. They seem to have a severe deficit in many of the higher-order abilities most people take for granted, such as setting life goals, making plans, and taking on and fulfilling responsibilities.

Jerry is a 37-year-old white male, although, like the border guards in West Germany, most people take him to be in his late 40s or early 50s. His IQ is above average, but his life seems to have little meaning or coherence. He appears to be unconcerned about the events of his life, and he also shows little emotion in his day-to-day existence. For example, he is not at all concerned by his lack of a permanent home, a steady job, companionship, or even a reasonably consistent source of food. He habitually withdraws from social situations, frequently wandering off from his home or job without any perceptible purpose or plan. When he does engage in conversation, his speech is vague and lacking in content, as illustrated by his intake interview at the VA hospital:

Therapist: Jerry, you left Salt Lake City about seven months ago, right?

Jerry: Yeah, I guess.

Therapist: So, what did you do during that time?

Jerry: Oh, I don't know. Different things I guess.

Therapist: Like what?

Jerry: You know, this and that. Nothing special.

Therapist: Well, like what? What did you do? Did you work?

Jerry: Oh, well, I did odd jobs. You know.

Therapist: What kind of odd jobs?

Jerry: Little things here and there.

Therapist: Like what? Can you think of any particular one?

Jerry: Um, yeah. I was a janitor for a while.

Therapist: How long did you do that?

Jerry: Not long.

Therapist: What's "not long"? A few days, weeks, months?

Jerry: A few days, I guess.

Therapist: Did you get paid for that?

Jerry: No, I don't think so.

Therapist: Well, how did you get money?

Jerry: Different ways.

Therapist: What kind of different ways?

Jerry: You know, odd jobs and stuff.

Therapist: Well, tell me this. How did you eat?

> Jerry: You know, garbage.
>
> (Later)

Therapist: Of all the places you were, where did you like it best?

Jerry: Arizona, I guess.

Therapist: Why Arizona?

Jerry: Oh, different reasons.

Therapist: Could you name one?

Jerry: Well, it's drier there.

Therapist: Do you mean it's less humid?

Jerry: No, not really.

Therapist: Well, what then?

Jerry: The ground's drier.

Therapist: What do you mean, "The ground is drier"?

Jerry: Well, there's less dew when you wake up.

Therapist: Oh, I see.

Jerry is also characterized by an almost complete absence of any emotional reaction. His blunted affect is illustrated by the following excerpt from the same interview:

Therapist: So, you were in an ambulance unit in Vietnam?

Jerry: Uh huh.

Therapist: Did you see any combat.

Jerry: Some.

Therapist: How often?

Jerry: A couple of times.

Therapist: How many times? Once, twice?

Jerry: I don't know. Ten or twelve, maybe.

Therapist: Could you describe what it was like?

Jerry: Oh, well, you know, lots of blood and stuff. Smoke. People yelling a lot. You know.

Therapist: Were you frightened?

Jerry: I guess so.

Therapist: What did you think about?

Jerry: Different things, nothing really. I just did my job.

Recollections of combat are very traumatic for most veterans. Either they are frightened and disturbed by the memories themselves, or they are bothered by the fact that these horrible memories do *not* disturb them. Jerry does not appear to have any kind of a reaction to these memories whatsoever. He tries to answer the questions as best he can, but his answers seem strangely distant and matter-of-fact.

Jerry's social withdrawal, his blunted affect, his peculiar lack of motivation or initiative, and his vague, uninformative speech all indicate the existence of a long-standing thought disorder that appears to have first emerged during his freshman year at college. At a concrete level, he understands his own behaviors and the behaviors of those around him, but he fails to grasp the meaning or purpose of these behaviors. This pervasive lack of comprehension and purpose, especially in the absence of any full-blown psychotic symptoms, characterizes someone suffering from Schizophrenia, Residual Type. Since his symptoms have existed for more than two years, his residual schizophrenia is categorized as chronic. (Patients with a history of psychotic symptoms of from six months' to two years' duration would be categorized as subchronic; those with shorter histories would not be diagnosed as schizophrenic.)

Jerry's history also includes occasional angry or agitated outbursts, such as beating down his door and harassing people in a park. These outbursts seem to indicate the emergence of active phases of Jerry's schizophrenic disorder. By the general descriptions of these outbursts, Jerry would probably be characterized as a disorganized or paranoid schizophrenic. However, the information available from Jerry's records is not detailed enough to determine accurately which of these labels is most appropriate, or even if they indicate an active phase at all. Since the active phases of Jerry's illness cannot be reliably classified, the most appropriate diagnosis for Jerry at his most recent hospitalization is Chronic Schizophrenia, Residual Type.

As is the case for most chronic schizophrenics, Jerry's treatment is primarily pharmacological. On admission to the VA hospital, he was given the phenothiazine chlorpromazine (known by the trade name Thorazine) at a standard maintenance dosage of 100 milligrams four times a day. This treatment regimen serves two purposes. First, it is intended to promote the highest possible level of Jerry's functioning by minimizing his residual symptoms. Second and perhaps more important, it is aimed at preventing a reoccurence of an active phase of his disorder. Since Jerry's history includes only isolated instances of psychotic behavior, his therapists are confident that this maintenance dose will be effective in warding off the reemergence of any future active phase. Patients who are presently in an active phase or who have a history of frequent decompensations generally are given higher doses.

In addition to receiving medication while he was in the hospital, Jerry also participated in various therapeutic activities designed to improve his social and occupational skills. On Tuesdays and Fridays, the patients and the therapeutic staff (therapists, interns, and nurses) of Jerry's ward would gather together for community meetings. To promote their sense of control and responsibility, the patients are put in charge of these meetings. One patient is chosen to be the discussion leader, another is chosen to act as the secretary —which entails organizing the proceedings and taking minutes. These biweekly community meetings allow the patients to raise issues and concerns in the presence of the entire ward and are intended to facilitate direct discussions among the patients and between the patients and staff. The primary focus of these discussions usually concerns practical issues on the ward (e.g., who is leaving/joining the ward, the policy on issuing day passes, information on field trips and events, etc.). The patients also participate in group therapy sessions. These sessions involve only a few patients at a time and are led by a single staff member. The object of these groups is to discuss interpersonal issues that are of concern to individual patients. The small size of these groups makes it possible for an individual patient's problems to be addressed thoroughly in open and frank discussions.

Like most of the patients, Jerry was not particularly interested in participating in either group activity. After a few weeks on the ward, however, Jerry was elected as the group secretary, an activity that had several positive, though indirect, effects. This activity forced him to interact with other patients in order to organize the meetings. He also had to review the minutes of the last session prior to reading them and pay closer attention during each meeting. These demands compelled Jerry to become more aware of the interpersonal aspects of living on the ward.

In group therapy Jerry's seeming indifference to social relationships was a prime topic. Jerry and his group leader set up a behavioral contract that reinforced him (through public recognition and added ward privileges) for spending time interacting with other patients and staff members. Jerry responded to this contingency almost immediately. Instead of spending most of his recreation time alone, he began to take long walks around the hospital grounds with other patients. He also became much more involved in ward outings and other special events. For example, during an observation visit by a group of graduate students, Jerry approached several students and struck up a conversation. He had a friendly attitude and was responsive to their questions, although the students found the actual content of his speech to be rambling and rather uninformative. Nevertheless, the staff asserted that even this limited approach behavior represented a big advance for Jerry.

Another aspect of Jerry's program involved limited vocational training. As the patients' symptoms begin to recede and become more manageable, they are enrolled in supervised workshops run by the hospital. Here they are trained to perform unskilled tasks (e.g., washing dishes, answering phones, etc.). Some patients are placed into semiskilled workshops. The therapeutic importance of this training is not in learning the vocational skills *per se* but in developing the discipline needed to hold a steady job. Jerry received carpentry training, and he presently works in the hospital's wood-finishing shop, where patients refurbish used or abandoned furniture that is then used by the hospital or sold to the public.

The next step in the program is to discharge the patients from the ward and set them up in semi-independent apartments, which are located in a complex about three miles from the hospital. Patients live in individual studio apartments and are responsible for their own food, laundry, transportation, and entertainment. The rent of the apartments is controlled, and the hospital can arrange to pay a patient's rent directly if he or she proves to be incapable of doing so. In addition, the patients are supervised by a staff member who lives in the apartment complex.

After six weeks on the ward, Jerry moved into his apartment. He works at the wood-finishing shop three days a week and attends group therapy once a week. He has had no problems taking public buses to the hospital, and his attendance, both at work and at group therapy, has remained good (around 90%). He seems to have no problem in performing his personal errands such as shopping and doing his laundry. One month after moving into his apartment, Jerry's medication was reduced to 200 milligrams per day; for the past eight months he has been maintained on this relatively low dose and appears to be doing well. Jerry's only particularly noticeable symptom is his persistent disinterest in forming interpersonal relationships.

❑ PROGNOSIS

On the whole, Jerry seems to be functioning well in his structured job and sheltered living situation. Many of his more pronounced residual symptoms (e.g., his inability to feed and clothe himself, his unwillingness to stay at a job, etc.) have declined as he has developed a more steady, normal routine. In all likelihood, though, Jerry will need to continue living in a fairly sheltered environment and taking his medication to maintain these thera-peutic gains and prevent a reoccurrence of his more serious psychotic symptoms. As is the case with most chronic schizophrenics, getting Jerry to continue taking his medication is the key to his prognosis. Provided he remains in his supervised apartment and continues to take his antipsychotic medication, there is little reason to believe that Jerry's level of functioning will change significantly in the foreseeable future. Although his treatment has enabled him to live somewhat independently and even to be productive, there is little chance that Jerry will ever become truly autonomous. Thus his prognosis is poor, and the goal of treatment, like that of most chronic schizophrenics, is continued maintenance, not cure.

☐ DISCUSSION

The schizophrenias constitute a diverse class of disorders that progress through distinct phases and manifest themselves in a variety of ways. To make matters even more complex, schizophrenics show great individual differences in their behavior patterns. Some will show residual symptoms almost continuously and will decompensate into an active phase only rarely, if ever. Some will display a single, acute psychotic episode without a reoccurrence. Still others will cyclically alternate between episodes of mild, residual symptoms and florid, psychotic behavior. Furthermore, psychiatric professionals have found it very difficult, if not impossible, to predict when a particular patient will enter an active phase. Thus estimates of the percentage of schizophrenics who fall into each of these groups at any given time vary widely, and reliable figures are not available at the present time. However, most researchers agree that the majority of schizophrenics exhibit residual symptoms most of the time, and these symptoms are the most commonly observed signs of the disorder. Interestingly, the public perception of schizophrenia seems to be based mostly on the psychotic symptoms that emerge during the active phase of the disorder. While these bizarre and seemingly "crazy" behaviors are very vivid, they are less frequently observed than are the more mild residual symptoms. This is particularly true since the majority of schizophrenics who demonstrate severe psychotic symptoms are quickly separated from the public and brought to psychiatric wards and institutions. In short, although the psychotic behavior evident during the active stage of schizophrenia is representative of the public's perceptions of the disorder, in reality the residual symptoms of schizophrenia are much more common.

At present little is known about the causes of schizophrenia, and so far therapists have not been successful in developing a cure for this disorder.

However, a number of antipsychotic drugs, first prescribed in the 1950s, have proven to be very effective in eliminating the overt, psychotic behavior demonstrated in the active phase. In contrast, these drugs have had only a limited effect on patients' residual symptoms. Thus treatment for schizophrenics is primarily through the administration of antipsychotic medication with the goal of decreasing their psychotic symptoms and controlling their residual symptoms to a point where they can function at a more manageable and productive level. Most schizophrenic patients, at least during the initial stages of their treatment, are prescribed one of the phenothiazines (Thorazine, Stelazine, or Mellaril) because of their relatively mild side effects. If this proves ineffective, the patient is then switched to a butyrophenone such as haloperidol (Haldol).

When prescribing antipsychotic medication, psychiatrists must keep several issues in mind. First, the dosage is carefully monitored to correspond to the patient's needs. Patients who are in the midst of an active phase are given a relatively large dose (up to 1,200 mg. per day of Thorazine, for example) to counteract their blatantly psychotic behavior. As these symptoms subside, their medication is gradually reduced to a maintenance level. Some patients will show notable improvement in their residual symptoms while at a maintenance level; their dosage may be further reduced. Occasionally, a patient will not show any residual signs following the abatement of his or her psychotic symptoms. In these rare cases the patient is not likely to suffer a psychotic break in the near future and may be withdrawn from medication entirely. However, the majority of patients will be kept at a maintenance level to control their residual symptoms and prevent a decompensation to a future active phase.

A second consideration in prescribing antipsychotic medication is making sure the patients actually take their medication. Most patients who take antipsychotic medication suffer some side effects, including nausea, grogginess, and irritability. Without supervision, most schizophrenics discontinue their medication soon after they are released. Subsequently they slowly decompensate back to an active phase, and at this point they are readmitted for treatment and again given antipsychotic medication. This cycle of treatment and decompensation has become known as the "revolving-door syndrome." The problem has become more widespread as the number of available psychiatric beds declines, limiting most facilities to short-term pharmacological treatment.

Sometimes a patient's odd cognitions, in and of themselves, may interfere with pharmacological treatment. One case, for example, involved a paranoid schizophrenic's delusions concerning Mellaril tablets, which are green, yellow, or pink, depending on the dosage. This patient refused to take any green pills, saying they were poisoned. As a result the staff had to make sure to keep a supply of pink Mellaril tablets available.

A third consideration is for therapists to be aware of other medications or drugs the patient may also be taking. The home environments of many patients, especially those in poor urban areas, commonly include alcohol and illicit drugs. Sometimes friends or family members even attempt to smuggle drugs into the psychiatric wards. As much as possible, the staff must avoid prescribing medication that may have an adverse, or even lethal, interaction with other substances.

Despite these limitations, pharmacological therapy remains the most effective treatment for the schizophrenias. Other treatments—including behavior therapy and traditional psychodynamic therapy—have been attempted, but they are largely ineffective—at least until the florid psychotic symptoms are first controlled. Residential programs that provide schizophrenics with a sheltered environment that insulates them from daily pressures and hassles seem to provide some gains over pharmacological therapy alone. Thus a combination of antipsychotic medication and a sheltered environment appears to be the best method now available for fostering at least a minimal level of functioning and preventing the onset of future active phases.

Jerry received a very comprehensive treatment that effectively combined these two elements. Jerry's treatment was atypical in that he was able to benefit from the outstanding facilities of the particular VA program he entered. The vast majority of treatment programs for schizophrenics do not possess comparable facilities; most are short-term programs that can afford to treat only the most severely psychotic schizophrenics—and then only on a "crisis management" basis. Because of a lack of sheltered housing, patients whose overtly psychotic symptoms have subsided after a few weeks are often simply released. In many cases these schizophrenics have no steady home or family, and they just wander the streets until their next active phase emerges. For most schizophrenics, this revolving-door syndrome will predominate for the rest of their lives.

PRIMARY DEGENERATIVE DEMENTIA OF THE ALZHEIMER TYPE: SENILE ONSET

Supportive Therapy

❑ PRESENTING COMPLAINT

Emma is a 74-year-old woman who lives alone in a medium-sized town in central Indiana. She has been widowed for six years. Her daughter and son-in-law also live in this town, and they visit her often, usually two or three times a week.

Approximately two months ago Emma and her daughter went on a shopping trip to Indianapolis. Emma seemed to enjoy the ride to the city, and she and her daughter engaged in friendly, although somewhat vacuous and disorganized, conversation. When they arrived downtown, Emma became very confused. She did not know where she was or why she was there. She asked seemingly foolish questions, such as, "What's the name of this place?" and "Why are you taking me here?" She became very upset and asked her daughter to take her home again. Her daughter was very much surprised by the extent of her mother's disorientation, and she tried to explain where they were and the purpose of the trip. Emma continued to be confused, however. Seeing little use in continuing the outing, they drove home.

When they returned to Emma's house, her daughter noticed other signs that something was wrong with her mother. Emma had left her stove on, and she had also left a pan with scrambled eggs in the refrigerator. She could not say how long the stove had been on or when she had put the pan in the refrigerator; in fact, she had no memory of having made scrambled eggs or of having eaten breakfast that morning. She became very upset, and after a few minutes she became angry and refused to answer her daughter's questions. She then asked her daughter to leave.

That evening the daughter called to ask if Emma was feeling ill. Emma said no and asked her daughter why she thought so. She had only a vague memory of their trip. She did not recall the conversation or the argument they had had that morning.

The next day Emma was taken to see her physician. He found nothing physically wrong with her. He did notice, however, that she appeared to remember very little about recent events and seemed somewhat disoriented during the examination. He then referred her for a more detailed mental status examination at the neurology clinic of the local hospital. Emma was given a battery of diagnostic tests, including a CT (computerized axial tomography) scan, an EEG (electroencephalogram), and various blood tests. After analyzing the results of these tests, the neurologist found evidence of cortical atrophy and nonspecific, bilateral brainwave slowing. He was noncommittal about his diagnosis, but he mentioned the possibility of Alzheimer's disease. Emma's daughter and son-in-law were dissatisfied with this diagnosis and sought a second opinion. They were referred to a neurology clinic in Indianapolis.

❑ PERSONAL HISTORY

Emma's daughter and son-in-law drove her to the neurology clinic in Indianapolis. Emma appeared confused and nervous, and her daughter provided Emma's history.

Emma was born in Chicago, the daughter of Swedish immigrants who came to Illinois at the turn of the century. Emma is the second-oldest of six children: two boys and four girls. She had an eighth-grade education and worked as a store clerk in Chicago until her marriage. When she was 40 she took a job as a teller at a local bank. In accordance with company policy, she retired when she was 65.

Emma's medical history is unremarkable. She is described by her daughter as a "light social drinker." She has not smoked in over forty years. She has no history of any head injury, thyroid disease, or any other serious medical problem. Fifteen years ago she had cataract surgery without any complications.

The medical history of Emma's family is somewhat unclear. Her parents died over twenty years ago, and her daughter cannot recall the causes of their deaths. Her husband had a history of coronary disease and died six years ago from cardiac arrest. One brother was diagnosed as having Alzheimer's disease before he passed away; her other siblings are still alive.

According to her daughter, Emma suffers from "minor mood problems" involving occasional feelings of anxiety and depression. Fifteen months ago she was prescribed the tricyclic antidepressant doxepin (Sinequan), and she continues to take a very small maintenance dose of 30 milligrams per day. Other than this, Emma has no history of any psychiatric disorder. She is not on any other medication.

Asked to describe Emma's "minor mood problems" in more detail, the daughter replied:

> Mom was fine until a couple of years ago. She had been living
> alone for about four years. About this time she started staying
> home a lot. She didn't seem to want to go out much, even to visit
> friends, and she started calling us less often. She seemed to get
> angry and irritable with other people much easier than she used
> to. She also starting getting confused about things—where she
> kept different things around the house and who she talked to, that
> sort of thing. This was all pretty gradual. Lately she's been very
> hesitant to do things on her own. It seems that I take her just
> about everywhere now: shopping, to the beauty parlor, to the
> bank. I told you about the shopping trip.
>
> About a year ago we took her to a gerontology specialist. We
> told him what we had been noticing, but he didn't seem to know
> what was wrong. He gave her medication for her anxiety, though.
> She still takes it, but it doesn't seem to help much; she seems to
> be getting worse lately. As you know, we saw another neurologist
> two weeks ago, but he also didn't seem to know what was wrong.

❏ CONCEPTUALIZATION AND TREATMENT

Emma's failing memory and increasingly frequent periods of profound disorientation suggest that she is suffering from a progressive dementia. According to *DSM-III-R*, dementia (what most lay people would call "senility") is a condition marked by a significant impairment in higher cortical function or change in personality. Characteristic symptoms include feelings of confusion and disorientation in familiar settings, memory loss, difficulty in maintaining concentration, impairment in one's ability to exercise good judgment and think abstractly, and an increase in irritability or aggression. In many cases there may be evidence of paranoid delusions and hallucinations, aphasia (disruptions in the ability to use or understand language), agnosia (inability to recognize familiar objects or events), and apraxia (difficulty in carrying out coordinated actions such as cooking or dressing).

Several neurological tests have been developed to measure the extent of a person's dementia. One is the Blessed Test. The Blessed Test is a thirty-three-item questionnaire that assesses a patient's functioning in the following areas: knowledge of common, everyday facts (e.g., the patient's name, the time and date, the present location, etc.), memory (e.g., place of birth, names of family members, names of recent Presidents, etc.), and concentration (e.g., adding two numbers, counting backward, etc.). The patient scores one point for every question he or she cannot answer correctly. Thus the higher the score on this test, the more extensive the cognitive impairment.

Emma scored 24 on the Blessed Test. She was able to state her name and her place of birth, and she knew the names of close family members. However, she failed at tasks that made use of less personal information. She did not know the correct date, the day of the week, or the month. She could not say where she was, or even that she was in a hospital. She could not name any presidents. She could not recall an address or a series of numbers given to her five minutes before (or even that they were given to her). She was also unable to count backward. When she was asked to add 8 and 5, she appeared confused and copied these numbers over and over.

Emma's responses on this test show that she suffers from moderate to severe impairment in her cognitive abilities. This finding is not wholly surprising, considering her daughter's description of her odd behavior. Another factor consistent with this result is her age. Whereas dementia is rare for persons under 50, the prevalence of this disorder climbs quickly as age increases. Roughly 4 percent of Americans over 65 suffer from some form of dementia, and by age 80 the figure is over 20 percent. Studies report that more than half of the dementia cases are of the Alzheimer Type.

Dementia of the Alzheimer Type, commonly referred to as Alzheimer's disease, is a form of dementia marked by an insidious onset and a gradual, but inexorable deterioration in a multitude of intellectual abilities. Memory, judgment, and decision-making processes are affected, and personality changes may be noticed. Agitation and irritability are common, and paranoid delusions and hallucinations may be present. In time, the ability to perform even simple tasks is impaired, and eventually these patients are no longer able to care for themselves.

Alzheimer's disease is a progressive, degenerative neurological condition. Like other forms of dementia, Alzheimer's disease is characterized by a general cerebral atrophy (wasting away), which can be identified by CT and

NMR (nuclear magnetic resonance) scans. However, this is not an absolute indication of the disease; cerebral atrophy can also occur in cognitively normal subjects. Another nonspecific finding in dementia is an EEG showing slow, diffuse patterns. Unfortunately, specific abnormalities that may indicate Alzheimer's disease (i.e., the existence of senile plaques and neurofibrillary bundles) can be detected only by brain biopsy, which is used for premorbid diagnosis of Alzheimer's disease only in extraordinary cases where there is a good possibility of finding another treatable cause of dementia.

Given a patient history of dementia with an insidious onset and a gradual progression, an ultimate diagnosis of Alzheimer's disease is probable once all other known causes of dementia (stroke, chronic alcohol abuse, etc.) have been ruled out. At this point a *DSM-III-R* diagnosis of Primary Degenerative Dementia of the Alzheimer Type is made. When symptoms manifest themselves before age 65, the disorder is said to have a Presenile Onset; when symptoms first emerge after age 65, a Senile Onset is indicated.

Emma's neurologist found no evidence for any other known etiology of her symptoms. The failure to identify a specific cause of her disorder, combined with the insidious onset and the gradual but steady progression of her symptoms, led him to conclude that the chances were about 90 percent that she suffered from Alzheimer's disease.

At the present time there is no known treatment for the primary symptoms of this disorder, and the only help available for Emma and her family is supportive therapy. This therapy has several purposes. First, it can inform the patient and his or her family what the disease is and what they can expect in terms of functioning. Second, this therapy can suggest several "tricks" to aid the patient's memory and concentration, thus prolonging his or her ability to function independently. Third, this therapy gives both the patient and the family a place to air frustrations and complaints. Lastly, and perhaps most important, this therapy helps the patient, and especially the family, to cope with the relentless progression of this disorder.

Immediately after Emma's diagnosis, she and her daughter began meeting with a counselor from the hospital once a week. Gradually these meetings became less frequent, until they were held approximately once a month. These sessions provided Emma with an empathic listener with whom she could share her doubts, fears, and frustrations. Emma also found her counselor to be a useful sounding board for her complaints, especially those concerning her daughter.

The counselor also provided Emma and her daughter with some specific "tricks" to help them cope with Emma's impaired memory and judgment. First, the counselor suggested that other people ask Emma direct, "recognition" questions instead of "recall" questions. The counselor explained that often memory is aided when a person is asked to decide whether a given event is true or not (recognition) rather than having to regenerate the event from scratch (recall). For example, Emma found it easier to answer a question such as "Did you have eggs or cereal for breakfast?" instead of "What did you have for breakfast?" Similarly, "Was that Gladys on the phone?" was easier to answer than "Who was that on the phone?"

A second set of tricks was designed to reduce Emma's increasing confusion about her routine, everyday tasks. To help Emma remember to perform these minor chores, her daughter put labels around the house. Thus a label on Emma's nightstand read "Take your pill," to remind her to take her medication at bedtime. Labels near the door also reminded her to lock the door and to turn off the stove. Since Emma forgot which light switches turned on which lights, her daughter labeled each switch with its target: "Hall Light," "Kitchen Light," "Porch Light," and so on. As Emma's aphasia worsened, she gradually lost her ability to recognize the words on these labels. At this point her daughter, with a fair amount of ingenuity, added pictures to many of the labels.

Third, since Emma often lost her place in the middle of doing her chores or errands, she (or more often her daughter) wrote out directions for various everyday tasks. For instance, the particular steps involved in doing the laundry or taking out the garbage were written out in detail. Emma found it easier to complete these tasks if she had some concrete set of directions to refer to when she forgot her place in the sequence of steps.

Supportive counseling can be of as much benefit to the families of Alzheimer patients as to the patients themselves. In Emma's case, her daughter was particularly slow to accept the fact that her mother had developed a gradual, terminal disease. One indication of her denial was the great discrepancy between her description of her mother's behaviors and Emma's performance at the examination. The daughter reported that Emma suffered from "getting confused" and "minor mood problems." In contrast, Emma's Blessed Test score of 24 provides evidence of considerable cognitive impairment at that time. Another indication of the daughter's denial was her refusal to accept the findings of Emma's first neurological examination. In the neurologist's words, "I get the distinct impression that Emma's daughter just refuses to believe that her mother has Alzheimer's disease." After she finally did accept this diagnosis, she became able to care for her mother in a more constructive way. She became more aware of the many signs of her mother's dementia. She was able to be more patient and caring with her mother, and much of her frustration at her mother's illogical behaviors evaporated. She set up the various memory "tricks" around Emma's home. She also made an effort to explain Emma's condition to friends, who had been surprised by the mother's apathetic and sometimes hostile attitude. She decided to take over

Emma's financial affairs as well. Finally, and most important, she became able to accept the fact of her mother's gradual and unavoidable deterioration.

☐ PROGNOSIS

The course of this disease is one of gradual, progressive cortical deterioration. Cognitive impairments such as memory loss and disorientation become increasingly pervasive. Typically the patient also experiences more frequent periods of agitation and apathy as the disorder worsens. The patient may withdraw almost completely from social interactions. In severe cases the patient will experience difficulties in walking and may become bedridden. Eventually the patient may lose his or her ability to perform even the most routine task and may require constant supervision. Only a minority of patients with Alzheimer's disease die as a direct result of their dementia; however, their prolonged illness makes them especially vulnerable to medical problems that may not have taken their lives otherwise (e.g., cardiovascular disease, pneumonia, etc.). The duration of Alzheimer's disease is poorly documented. The limited evidence that is available indicates that the length of the illness varies widely between individual patients. For any particular case, the duration of the illness depends in large measure on how alert the patient's family is to his or her condition and how quickly they respond when medical problems do arise.

Six months after her visit to the clinic in Indianapolis, Emma was unable to recall the majority of recent events, most noticeably conversations she had had with her family or friends. She was frequently disoriented and increasingly had great difficulty linking individual actions into purposeful behaviors. One by one she gave up her friendships (usually because she failed even to recognize her friends and acquaintances), and she gradually became more irritable around her daughter.

After a year she was brought back to the neurologist in Indianapolis and given a follow-up examination. As he predicted, her deterioration was marked. She now scored 31 on the Blessed Test. She was able to provide only her name and place of birth, and she did not understand most other questions.

After another year her cognitive functioning had deteriorated to the point where she was unable to care for herself. She could no longer dress or wash herself and was frequently incontinent. At this point, Emma's daughter was spending virtually all her time at her mother's home. With the encouragement of her husband and her counselor, the daughter finally decided to place Emma in a nursing home. There Emma's cognitive abilities continued to deteriorate, and she died of pneumonia approximately a year later.

☐ DISCUSSION

Emma's case is fairly typical. The insidious onset of her cognitive impairment, the gradual progression of her symptoms, her deepening social withdrawal and irritability, and finally her complete loss of the ability to care for herself are all sadly common. In some rare cases Alzheimer's disease strikes people in their late 40s or 50s. In most cases, however, as with Emma, the disorder affects people late in life (in their 70s or 80s).

Another typical aspect of this case was the daughter's resistance to acknowledging her mother's disorder. Because of the insidious onset of Alzheimer's disease, few family members notice any abrupt behavioral changes. However, most do notice memory impairment and disorientation, which are frequently accepted as part of "growing old." Because of the difficulty patients and family members have in accepting a diagnosis of Alzheimer's disease, supportive therapy is especially important.

The specific causes of Alzheimer's disease are unknown. The neurological degeneration involved in this disorder may be detected in CT and NMR scans and in EEGs (although often these test results are normal, especially during the early phases of the disease). Unfortunately, these gross neurological signs are also found in other organic brain disorders, and their presence is not an automatic indication of Alzheimer's disease. At the present time there are no tests that prove the existence of Alzheimer's disease; this diagnosis is warranted only after all other known causes of dementia have been ruled out. It is particularly important to rule out forms of dementia that are potentially reversible (e.g., chronic alcohol or drug use, subdural hematoma [stroke], etc.) so that the patient may receive treatment. Other forms of dementia, which may be treatable to some extent (e.g., Multi-infarct dementia, Parkinson's disease, etc.), must also be ruled out.

Because of the obvious physiological base of the patients' symptoms and the need to rule out competing diagnoses, the focus in these cases is almost exclusively on the medical and neurological aspects of the patients' histories. As a result, factors that would be ignored in most psychiatric evaluations are of vital importance; patient histories tend to be limited to past diseases, surgeries, physical traumas, medication, and psychiatric disorders. In particular, factors that may support a competing diagnosis (e.g., high blood pressure, hypothyroidism, a history of depression) are investigated closely. Little weight is given to subjective experiences; in fact, in most cases histories are provided by family members and not by the patients themselves.

Attention is paid to personal feelings, concerns, or memories only to the extent that they may provide information about the existence (or the extent) of the patients' dementia. Since no medical or psychological cure for this disorder is known, in most cases therapy is limited to supportive counseling for the patients and their families.

Alzheimer's disease is a profoundly disturbing and frightening experience for the patient, and taking care of someone with Alzheimer's disease is an emotionally and physically taxing responsibility, particularly if the patient is a close relative. For these reasons, supportive therapy is very important, perhaps more so for the families of these patients than for the patients themselves. First, the families are informed of the causes, the symptoms, and the predicted course of the disease. In fact, giving the families an idea of what to expect appears to be as valuable as any other aspect of this therapy. The family members are also reminded that the patients are not willfully acting in a difficult or forgetful manner; their behavior is to a great extent involuntary. This knowledge often helps the family members remain patient and calm in particularly trying situations.

Another common problem is that in many cases family members take on the entire responsibility for the care of these patients. Some report feeling a great sense of duty to the patient (who is usually a spouse or parent) and avoid being away from them, even briefly, lest some unfortunate accident or mishap should occur. As the patient becomes more impaired, the caretaker finds it increasingly difficult to meet the demands of his or her own life while looking after the constant needs of the patient. Feelings of frustration and resentment are common, as are pangs of guilt. Typically the central focus of counseling at this stage of the disorder is to address these very issues. Family members are told not to let the patient's needs disrupt their own lives. If the patient degenerates to the point where constant care is necessary, they are encouraged to accept this fact and either hire a private nurse or companion, or place the patient in a nursing home. Institutionalizing a patient, particularly a spouse or parent, is a very stressful and difficult decision, and supportive therapy aids the caretakers in coming to grips with this painful issue and with the patient's eventual death.

SEPARATION ANXIETY DISORDER WITH A MAJOR DEPRESSIVE EPISODE

Psychodynamic Therapy

❏ PRESENTING COMPLAINT

Eve is a 10-year-old fifth-grader who lives in a middle-class suburb of Chicago. In February, Eve contracted pneumonia and was kept home for two weeks. During this time she had the undivided attention of her mother. The day before Eve was scheduled to return to school, she complained of severe abdominal pain, so severe that she could barely walk, let alone go to school. She was taken to the emergency room of the local hospital, but the physician on call could find nothing wrong with her. Still, she complained of a fever (though her parents could find no indication of any), headaches, and diarrhea, and she was allowed to stay home one week longer. Throughout the week Eve's complaints persisted, and her parents took her to her pediatrician three times. However, neither the parents nor the pediatrician could find any objective evidence of physical illness; her temperature was normal, she did not cough or have any difficulty breathing, and her appetite and sleep seemed good. On the recommendation of Eve's doctor, her parents now insisted that she return to school. Eve flatly refused. She began throwing tantrums and having "yelling matches" with her mother. She carried on for hours, complaining that she still was not feeling well and that she should not be forced to go back to school when she was so sick. She accused her mother of being selfish and neglectful and of "just wanting to get rid of (her)." In the mother's own words, "It's been pure bedlam ever since she refused to go back to school."

According to her mother, Eve had always been a dependent and demanding child, but she had never acted out to this extent before. Her mother became increasingly alarmed at and frustrated with Eve's uncharacteristic behavior. Although Eve did not carry on in front of her father in the way she did with her mother, he nevertheless became very concerned about her refusal to go back to school. After a fourth week of staying home, Eve's parents decided to contact a local psychiatrist who specialized in childhood disorders.

Eve's mother took her to her initial interview at the psychiatrist's office. The mother was asked to remain in the waiting room while Eve described how she felt about what had happened during the last few weeks. Eve was uncharacteristically self-disclosing for a girl her age; she began the interview by saying, "OK. Let's start at the beginning."

From Eve's viewpoint her problem was much more involved than just refusing to go to school. At first she complained that she was still sick with a fever of "almost 100" and diarrhea. (Most likely, the diarrhea was a side effect of the medication she was still taking for her pneumonia.) She was very angry with both her mother and her pediatrician for trying to make her go back to school. She complained that they did not appreciate how sick she felt and did not take her seriously. As she stated, "They just don't understand me. Whatever I say is a joke. I mean, what would happen if I got *really* sick?" Her psychiatrist then asked her to describe these feelings in more detail, but Eve interrupted him, saying, "I'm not done yet!" She then went on to describe a second problem:

> My mind thinks ahead. It's like my mind gets ahead of me. Every
> time something good happens to me, I think ahead to the bad
> things that may happen afterwards. It's like a state of shock or
> fright. Sometimes I'm afraid my mom will get killed or the house
> will burn down or something. This happens at school a lot. I wish
> I could jump out the window and be home to help. When it (the
> "fright") happens, I mostly want to be at home where someone
> can take care of me.

Eve was obviously very upset by what she called her "fright," but she could not specify any particular cause for her anticipatory anxiety. She denied that anything or anyone bothers her at school; she said that she has several good friends and that her schoolwork is very easy. The only truly consistent aspect of her "fright" is her strong desire to be home, a place she describes as "secure and full of protecting people."

Eve also told her psychiatrist that she feels "sadness and madness" most of the time. She described this feeling as "crying inside" and said that she actually cries frequently, usually for no reason. She also said that she often wakes up around 2 o'clock in the morning because of her "fright" and has trouble getting back to sleep. As mentioned above, this "fright" primarily involves her morbid preoccupations that she or her family members may develop terrible diseases or be injured or killed.

Suicidal ideation is quite rare in children Eve's age, and usually this topic is not discussed in therapy. However, Eve's psychiatrist thought it prudent to ask her if she had ever thought of killing herself. She said that she had wished to be dead on many occasions, and she would often tell her mother that she was going to commit suicide. She would even make "fake" suicide attempts. For example, two days before her interview she emptied a bottle of aspirin and left it where her mother would be sure to find it. She then locked herself in the bathroom with the faucet running. She said that her mother was very frightened and pounded on the bathroom door for several minutes before Eve finally opened it. She claimed that she would never actually go through with a suicide attempt; she just wants to know that her mother cares.

Eve also reported hearing voices, which usually said terrible things. She remembers that one time the voices said that she was a very bad girl and needed to die. She said that some voices seemed to come from inside her head whereas others seemed to come from outside. Occasionally there would be an argument between the voices inside and outside her head. Eve was very frightened by these voices and wanted them to "just go away." She realized that these voices were quite odd; in fact, she said that she felt nervous just talking about them.

Finally, the psychiatrist asked her if she had any problems getting along with her friends, with the other kids at school, or with her family. Eve denied any interpersonal problems. She apparently got along well with her friends at school, and she seemed to have fairly normal relationships with her two sisters. She said she respected and admired her father, and aside from disliking the fact that he wanted her to go back to school, she had a good relationship with him. She did, however, complain of problems with her mother. Interestingly, these problems stemmed from the fact that she and her mother were too much alike.

Therapist: So, Eve, can you tell me about the troubles you have with your mother?

Eve: She's just like me; we're exactly alike. We're both yellers and screamers, and we have screaming matches all the time.

Therapist: Do you like your mom or do you dislike her?

Eve: Oh, I really like her.

Therapist: Eve, let's pretend you were giving your mom a grade on a pretend report card, OK? What grade would you give her?

Eve: A B. No, a B+.

Therapist: B+, OK. Why a B+?

Eve: Well, she helps me most of the time, and she's good to me, so I gave her a good grade.

Therapist: Why not an A?

Eve: Because she yells at me and jumps to too many conclusions.

❑ PERSONAL HISTORY

Eve grew up in a traditional, Protestant, middle-class family. Her father is a middle-level business executive, and he appears to be responsible and concerned about Eve. He spends time with his children on weekends, but because of his busy work schedule his interactions with them during the week are limited to dinner conversations. Her mother has never been employed outside the home; she says that she spends most of her time and effort taking care of her children and worrying about their welfare. Eve has two sisters, one older and one younger. Their relationships with one another seem to be fairly normal for children their age; they get into occasional arguments and shouting matches, but on the whole they get along well.

Eve's early childhood appears to be unremarkable. Her mother could think of nothing unusual about it, and her medical records show no indication of any serious or unusual injuries or illnesses. At age 4, Eve was enrolled in a nursery school that was held for half a day, three days a week. Transportation to and from the nursery school was provided by a car pool organized by some of the parents. Eve's mother remembers that Eve was very reluctant to go into the cars of other parents in the car pool. In kindergarten, the next year, Eve was picked up by a school bus. In contrast to her uncertainty about taking rides in strangers' cars, she apparently loved the bus rides, and until now she has had no other school-related problems. However, Eve's extracurricular relationships with her peers did contain some early signs of her separation anxiety. For example, since kindergarten Eve has attended day camp during the summers. Although she has always enjoyed these experiences, she has steadfastly refused to attend an overnight summer camp. Similarly, Eve avoids any overnight stays with friends. Once, in second grade, Eve was invited to a slumber party for one of her close friends. According to Eve, all her friends were to attend the party, and she "had to go." On the afternoon of the slumber party, however, Eve complained of severe leg pains—so severe that she could not walk. Her mother took her to an orthopedist that afternoon. The orthopedist could find nothing wrong with her legs, but he nevertheless recommended that she not attend the party as a precaution. This leg pain has reemerged off and on in the past years. Eve's mother reports that it seems to intensify when she (the mother) is away and recede when she returns home.

The psychiatrist also interviewed Eve's parents to identify any significant aspects of their histories. Eve's mother reports that a particularly noteworthy event occurred when she was 19. She was found to be at fault in a boating accident that nearly killed her mother (Eve's grandmother), and she confesses that she has felt guilty and responsible for her mother's welfare ever since. She also appears to be quite worried about her father. She stated to the therapist that her father has always had a heart condition and she has worried about this for years. She says that in the back of her mind she is "constantly waiting for the phone call."

Although Eve's father appears to be very responsible and concerned for his daughter's welfare, he is personally resistant to the idea of therapy. He has met with the psychiatrist only once, and even then he seemed reluctant to disclose any information about himself. An examination of his medical records shows a history of depression in his family. When asked about this, he denies any history of mental illness in his family.

☐ CONCEPTUALIZATION AND TREATMENT

DSM-III-R defines Separation Anxiety Disorder as a child's excessive and unwarranted fear about being apart from his or her important attachment figures, usually the mother. This anxiety must have existed for at least two weeks. This disorder can be manifested through a number of symptoms, including unrealistic worries about the welfare of one's important attachment figures or one's own health, complaints of physical ailments and severe distress that would serve to prevent a separation from the attachment figures, persistent refusals to be separated from the attachment figures, and a need to be in constant contact with the attachment figures.

Eve clearly fits the *DSM-III-R* criteria for Separation Anxiety Disorder.

For the past few weeks she has exhibited excessive anxiety about being apart from her mother. She refuses to go to school and instead expresses a strong need to stay home. She complains of numerous physical ailments (headaches, abdominal pains, leg aches, etc.) and shows excessive distress when she is separated, or even anticipates being separated, from her mother. She persistently worries about her own health should she be separated from her mother ("What if I got *really* sick?"), and she has excessive worries that some terrible fate will befall the people close to her. As is the case with most children her age, Eve's Separation Anxiety Disorder is manifested primarily in her refusal to go to school or to allow any other situation that would separate her from her parents for any extended period of time.

Eve also shows symptoms of a Major Depressive Episode. She has complained of depressed mood and a lack of interest in her usual activities. She has complained of feelings of sadness and frustration, frequent crying, early morning awakening, various somatic complaints, mood-congruent hallucinations, and suicidal ideation. In fact, it is not uncommon for Separation Anxiety Disorder to co-occur with a Major Depressive Episode. Nevertheless, the severity of Eve's mood disorder is somewhat unusual for a child her age. The extent of her mood disturbance, combined with a family history of mood disorders, suggests the possibility that Eve may have a genetic predisposition toward depression.

Eve was diagnosed as having a Separation Anxiety Disorder with a Major Depressive Episode and was seen for therapy once a week at the psychiatrist's office. The psychiatrist ascribed Eve's symptoms to a neurotic fear that she would be abandoned and left alone. Much of her anxiety involved some catastrophic event that would make her parents, particularly her mother, unable to care for her. As Eve has grown she has been confronted with an increasing number of subtle demands for independence (e.g., slumber parties, summer camp, etc.), and recently it has become apparent that she is unable to cope with these demands.

Eve's treatment was aimed primarily at reducing the neurotic defenses that have inhibited her psychosocial development. Initially this goal was approached in three broad, progressive steps. First, Eve's pervasive anxieties, depressed mood, hallucinations, and suicidal ideation were brought under control, in part through medication. Second, her living situation, especially her relationship with her mother, was stabilized. Third, the psychiatrist worked with her mother to get Eve to return to school. After these initial steps, supportive therapy and psychodynamic therapy could proceed in earnest. Throughout treatment the psychiatrist provided Eve with emotional support, primarily by reassuring her that she was loved by her parents and that their frustrations and expectations were intended to be for her own good. In addition to this her psychodynamic therapy attempted to get her to understand her unconscious thoughts and feelings. As these were uncovered and discussed, the therapist provided Eve with clarifications, reinterpretations, and occasional confrontations.

The first concrete action taken by Eve's psychiatrist was to put her on the tricyclic antidepressant imipramine (known by the trade name Tofranil). Most children do not require medication; therapy usually consists of a combination of family intervention and situation manipulation (putting the child in situations that require a level of independence). However, in recent years imipramine has been found to be effective for children with more severe cases of this disorder, particularly cases involving school avoidance, and it is becoming more commonly prescribed in these cases.

Eve's initial dose of Tofranil was small. The dose was gradually increased until an appropriate blood level was achieved. This procedure provides the best chance of finding an efficacious and long-lasting dosage of medication while it minimizes the drug's negative side effects. Since Eve was only 10 years old, it was especially important to monitor closely her medication and her reactions to it (through frequent electrocardiograms, analyses of blood levels, etc.). After two and a half weeks on Tofranil, Eve's hallucinations and suicidal ideation ceased, her anxiety lessened, and her depressive symptoms began to remit. Eve was maintained on Tofranil throughout her therapy.

Another aspect of therapy involves treating the parents, or in this case, Eve's mother. The psychiatrist saw Eve's mother for several sessions. One goal of these sessions was to inform her of ways she could avoid unwittingly exacerbating Eve's problems. In particular, she was told to "just walk away" from the screaming matches she usually had with Eve and to extricate herself from Eve's problems as much as possible. She was also told to treat Eve with resolve and that the most effective way to get Eve to return to school was to be firm and stand her ground. Besides giving Eve's mother recommendations on how to interact with her daughter more effectively, a second purpose of these meetings was to emphasize to her that Eve's fears were very sincere and were not meant as a punishment. Eve's morbid preoccupations were not simply attempts to manipulate her parents; Eve actually feared for her own safety and the safety of her family. These fears may not have had a real (or even logical) basis, but they were nevertheless real to Eve. To emphasize this point, the psychiatrist informed Eve's mother of Eve's suicidal ideation and hallucinations. The mother quickly came to realize that Eve's anxieties were more serious and painful than she had initially thought. Similarly, Eve's frequent somatic complaints were not simply childish attempts at avoiding things (although they often did produce this effect); Eve really did feel pain. In short, Eve's parents were told that her fears were painful and sincere, even if they did not have any physiological base.

Four weeks after she began therapy, Eve returned to school, and she had no trouble catching up on her missed schoolwork. Gradually her relationship with her mother had become much more controlled; they argued less and Eve was more obedient. With Eve's return to school, therapy now focused on more dynamic issues. From this point Eve's psychotherapy was increased to twice a week. As indicated earlier, therapy focused on two primary goals: (1) to provide Eve with support and reassurance and (2) to uncover and interpret her unconscious thoughts and feelings.

First, Eve was reassured that her parents did indeed care for her. She was told that neither she nor they were in any actual serious danger and they would be available when she needed them. Eve's perceptions of her parents' demands on her (e.g., insisting she go to school, suggesting she attend summer camp, etc.) were also discussed. She was told to think of these expectations not as their wish to get rid of her but rather as signs that they really did care for her. They expected her to be a "big girl" who could take care of herself, and they wanted her to grow up and be successful. By and large Eve reacted favorably to these suggestions.

Second, the therapist attempted to uncover Eve's latent feelings. Like most children, Eve found it difficult to express such feelings directly, especially those that involved hostility or anxiety. As a result, psychodynamic therapy with Eve was conducted in a subtle and indirect manner. As the first step in this process, the therapist attempted to foster a close therapeutic alliance with Eve through the establishment of a nonerotic transference. ("Nonerotic" is used here in the oedipal sense and refers to the development of positive regard for the therapist. This differs from the transference frequently attempted with adults in that the therapist is seen as friendly and empathic but not specifically as a parental figure.) As the therapeutic alliance developed, Eve's unconscious perceptions of the people in her childhood began to be expressed in her current perceptions of the therapist. By carefully listening to and observing Eve, he helped her understand her perceptions of the world and distinguish her real experiences from her imagined ones. In the course of therapy, the therapist often attempted to have Eve "slip into" a discussion of her unconscious feelings through expressive play, where her feelings were projected onto the play situation. For example, Eve occasionally played with a dollhouse during the therapy sessions. During one session she placed a small doll next to a larger one and called the small one "Baby" and the larger one "Mommy." The therapist asked her what the baby was thinking. Eve replied, "The baby is very sad. She thinks that her mother is dying and that she'll be all alone." Eve's underlying cognitions were also expressed through art. During a later session, for example, Eve drew a picture of a starfish with a broken arm that appeared to be dangling from the rest of the creature. In the course of describing this picture to the therapist,

Eve commented that her family was like the starfish and that she herself was the broken appendage that was not really a part of the family. As therapy progressed the therapist was able (indirectly) to uncover and reinterpret many of the direct, core issues of Eve's problem, primarily her strong fears of abandonment. Since Eve's symptoms were thought to be a result of these underlying cognitions, therapy remained focused on these central issues and made no attempt to address her school avoidance per se.

An important aspect of conducting psychotherapy with children is to relate to them from their own "frame of reference." Therapists should attempt to match their techniques to the cognitive level of the children they treat and discuss issues that are important to these children. For example, when Eve's psychiatrist discussed "growing up" with her, he made sure to put this concept in terms that she would be able to understand. Whereas for older patients "growing up" might mean choosing a career or making life goals, for Eve "growing up" meant going to different rooms for different school subjects (instead of staying in the same home room) and having a locker of her own. As a second example, Eve's general desires and goals were given a concrete form by phrasing them as "birthday wishes." So, to tap Eve's hopes for the future, her psychiatrist asked, "What would you wish for on your next birthday?" Similarly, as described earlier, Eve was asked to give her mother a grade on a "pretend report card." Discussing topics at an abstract level usually surpasses a child's cognitive development and is less effective therapeutically than a more concrete approach.

After about six months, Eve's father suggested that her antidepressant medication be discontinued. Her depressive symptoms had long since remitted, and she appeared to be making slow but steady progress in overcoming her anxiety. Moreover, the process involved in monitoring her medication was very time consuming and expensive. In accord with her father's request, Eve was gradually withdrawn from Tofranil. However, within two weeks her depressive symptoms began to reappear. Eve was then put back on a maintenance dose of Tofranil, which she took until therapy was discontinued nine months later.

During the course of therapy, Eve's fears of separation gradually diminished. Her morbid preoccupations were rare, and her (much reduced) anxieties no longer interfered with her behavior. At this point Eve discontinued therapy. She still exhibited some mild "residual" signs of her disorder, such as a refusal to sleep over at friends' houses and a resistance to attending a full-time summer camp. However, most of her more incapacitating anxieties had long since remitted. Although her psychiatrist felt that Eve could have benefited from an additional year or so of therapy, the family's finances were such that continuing therapy was considered impractical, especially since only relatively small additional gains in functioning were anticipated.

☐ PROGNOSIS

Eve made good progress in her fifteen months of therapy; nevertheless, her prognosis is guarded. First, she has a family history of depression and had shown a reasonably full Major Depressive Episode by age 10. And although she responded well to imipramine, an interruption in her medication resulted in a reemergence of her symptoms. Taken together, this information indicates that Eve may have a genetic predisposition toward depression. In all likelihood she will remain vulnerable to depression throughout her life, and she may need to be medicated again if there are recurrent episodes.

A second cause for concern is that Eve has shown subtle signs that her disorder is persisting. Mostly her anxiety is manifested by her apprehension about being away from home for more than a few hours at a time; overnight outings are still out of the question. At the present time it is not known if Eve's subtle symptoms will continue to fade gradually or whether they will develop into a lifelong pattern of dependency.

In short, Eve has made substantial progress in therapy. The combination of antidepressant medication and psychodynamic therapy appears to have been very effective in reducing her defensive anxieties. Generally speaking, the prognosis for children with Separation Anxiety Disorder is good; approximately two-thirds show marked improvement. However, as is the case with Eve, the anxieties of most children with this disorder appear to be grossly, but not completely, resolved. Thus, it is not uncommon for these children to show some mild symptoms for many years.

☐ DISCUSSION

Eve's diagnosis was straightforward. Her pervasive fears clearly indicated a childhood anxiety disorder. Her symptomology—refusing to leave loved ones for any extended period, morbid preoccupations, and somatic complaints—was very typical of a child with Separation Anxiety Disorder. Some children show symptoms that were not manifested by Eve. Many have great difficulty in falling asleep without the major attachment figures. These children may demand to sleep in their parents' bed, or they may "camp out" by their parents' door. Some also complain of frequent nightmares involving their morbid ideation. A minority of these children cannot stand to be separated from their attachment figures for even brief periods. They either cling to them most of the day or constantly follow them around in what is known as "shadowing."

In considering Eve's diagnosis, her refusal to attend school might have been taken to indicate a phobia of the school situation. However, her lack of academic problems and her generally good relationships with her peers were indications that school was not a negative experience for her. Thus in her case, school avoidance appeared to be only a by-product of her separation anxiety and not a problem in and of itself.

An interesting aspect of this case is that Eve also suffered from a Major Depressive Episode. Her sadness, her suicidal ideation, her sleep disturbance (especially her early morning awakening, of which her parents apparently were unaware), and her frequent somatic complaints all support this additional diagnosis. The fact that she described hearing voices may be taken by some as evidence of a psychotic thought disorder such as Childhood Schizophrenia. However, these auditory hallucinations were wholly consistent with her depressed mood, and they did not exist in the absence of other depressive symptoms. In general, mood-congruent hallucinations that occur with a mood disorder are usually taken to be a symptom of the mood disorder and not an indication of a psychotic thought disorder. Eve also reported feeling frightened by these voices, and she realized that they were very odd. The fact that her hallucinations were not ego–syntonic (that is, they were not liked or accepted by Eve) is further evidence that a diagnosis of a psychotic thought disorder is in all likelihood unwarranted.

In interviews, most parents report some sort of subtle clues pointing to their children's Separation Anxiety Disorder. Some children seem shy with strangers, and some seem hesitant about leaving their parents. Other children are afraid of the dark or afraid of monsters, odd creatures, or large, fierce animals. Some children are very demanding, whereas others are overly compliant and obedient. The majority of these *post hoc* signs, however, are common in all children, regardless of whether they will develop an anxiety disorder. For example, in Eve's case it seemed significant to her mother that Eve was leery of other drivers in her nursery school car pool. However, at that age most children are afraid of entering strange people's cars (and rightly so). Thus it is very difficult to use parents' observations to predict which children may eventually develop this disorder. At present the only known valid indication of this disorder is that children whose parents had this disorder are more prone to developing it themselves.

Another difficulty in predicting this disorder is that its onset varies widely among different children. For some children the symptoms begin in early childhood; others show no signs of the disorder until college. Many children, like Eve, first develop their symptoms after coming down with a serious illness that forces them to rely on someone else (usually one or both parents). Many other children develop their symptoms after the death of a family member or some other catastrophe (a car accident, damage to the home from a violent storm, etc.). For yet others no such instigating event can be identified. One unifying element for all these children, though, is their sincere belief that they or their loved ones are in some sort of danger that could lead to a prolonged separation.

The course of this disorder also varies widely. Whereas some children will never show any renewed evidence of separation anxiety after their symptoms recede, others will show subtle "residual" signs of their excessive anxiety for many years. As was the case with their "predisposing" signs, different children will show these subtle "residual" signs in different ways. Many seem to function perfectly well throughout high school, but they become very worried about the prospect of going off to college, especially when this involves being far away from home. Other children with this disorder manage to go away to school, but they still feel a strong need to keep in contact. These children will either come home almost every weekend or call their parents frequently, some up to several times every day. In a few cases the disorder takes a chronic course. These children may never move far away from, or even out of, the family home. For them, continual contact with their parents—by living with them, visiting them frequently, or calling them several times a day—becomes a lifelong pattern.

Because the symptoms of these children often emerge as a result of their subjective fears and not as a result of any observable trauma, it is frequently difficult for other people to recognize or understand the gravity of their anxieties. In particular, parents often have great difficulty determining just what is making their children so fearful. Many parents simply think their children have overactive imaginations; others may accuse their children of being lazy or manipulative. Not surprisingly, as in the case of Eve, these attitudes are construed by the child as evidence of rejection, thus exacerbating their already strong separation anxieties. For this reason it is important for the parents to realize that their children's anxieties are unconsciously motivated. Children with somatic complaints really *do* feel pain; those with morbid preoccupations really *do* fear that their family will be harmed. While these anxieties may not be logical or reasonable, they are nevertheless real to the child.

Researchers have found that many children who develop a separation anxiety grow up in families that foster their needy, dependent behaviors. Many of these parents themselves have difficulties with separation; they may be overly involved with their children, overprotective, or just overworried. For example, during her recovery from pneumonia, Eve received her mother's "undivided attention," and each of Eve's many somatic complaints precipitated a trip to her pediatrician or the emergency room. During a session with the psychiatrist, Eve's mother admitted that she and her husband had never spent a night away from their children. From this information it seems clear that Eve's parents, particularly her mother, are overly-protective and cautious, and it is possible that they may have some unresolved separation issues of their own. Indeed, the mother's constant guilt and fear concerning her parents' health provides evidence of her own separation anxieties. As noted earlier, people who have had difficulties in establishing boundaries with their own parents are more apt to have children with anxiety disorders than are people who have not had such difficulties.

One interesting aspect of this disorder is the parents' decision of when to seek help for their child. Some parents have described feeling "choked" or "smothered" by the excessive demands of their children. Others become embarrassed when their child acts up in public or refuses to go to school or on extended outings. Of course, what constitutes "excessive" anxiety will vary from parent to parent. As discussed above, many parents tolerate or even promote a sense of anxious dependence on the part of their children. At some point, though, they decide that their child has become *too* anxious. Since most children with this disorder have a long history of dependent behavior, it is often unclear to therapists why parents bring their child to therapy when they do and not sooner. This ambiguity may be especially confusing for the child, who must decide how much dependence is appropriate and how much is too much.

Different therapies for Separation Anxiety Disorder have shown roughly similar results. The immature cognitive development of children this age prevents the therapist from treating them as adults. For traditional psychodynamic therapists, the aim of therapy is more to free these children from their defensive inhibition and facilitate future development than to help them achieve insight into their disorders. (In fact, at least according to some therapists, many adults also lack the cognitive maturity to achieve true insight into their disorders.) Similarly, behavior therapists find that these children lack the maturity and focus necessary to carry out many of the demands of their therapies, such as keeping detailed behavior logs or fulfilling behavior contracts. As a result, both approaches tend to have a relatively greater focus on support and encouragement. Thus the treatments derived from various theoretical approaches to this disorder (and to other childhood disorders) may differ less than they would for adult patients. In fact, the most profound differences seem to lie in the interpretations of the children's problems. Regardless of the theoretical orientation of the therapist, however, antidepressant medication is beginning to be commonly prescribed for Separation Anxiety Disorder, although many psychiatric professionals are very concerned about administering psychoactive drugs to children.

Psychodynamic interpretations of Separation Anxiety Disorder focus on the morbid preoccupations of these children. About one-half to three-fourths of the children with Separation Anxiety Disorder report a strong fear that they or a loved one may be injured or killed. Traditional psychodynamic theory has interpreted these anxieties as the children's projection of their unconscious hostile impulses against one or both parents. That is, after the oedipal drama these children were left with strong feelings of need and resentment toward their parents, particularly their mothers, engendering pathological mother-child relationships based on mutual hostile dependence. Since hostility toward attachment figures is unacceptable to the ego, these feelings were consequently projected onto other, less specific forces that might harm the parents (e.g., illnesses, accidents, storms, etc.). As these children mature, their hostile dependence on their mothers makes them unable to cope with the increased demands of independence.

More recent psychodynamic formulations have noted that many of the parents of children with this disorder are themselves needy and dependent. These neurotic traits probably indicate that these parents have unconscious unresolved issues involving their own parents. Thus it is possible that these children may have developed their anxieties as a result of their parents' neurotic behavior (e.g., a parent's reaction to a serious illness, a parent's threat of suicide, etc.). In addition, by identifying with their neurotic parents, these children may have developed a particularly weak conception of each parent. (This weak conception is often referred to as a fragile "internal structure" or a fragile "internal object.") Since the children's conception of their parent is so weak, they feel especially at risk of being abandoned and left alone.

Regardless of its underlying causes, Separation Anxiety Disorder remains a relatively common psychiatric disorder that afflicts different children in different ways. For the most part children respond well to treatment, and the younger the patient the better the prognosis. Untreated, this disorder may endure throughout the patient's life.

BULIMIA NERVOSA

Cognitive-Behavioral Therapy

☐ PRESENTING COMPLAINT

Jill is an attractive, blonde, 25-year-old woman who works as flight attendant for a major airline. She initially consulted her doctor (an internist) for help concerning recent periods of weakness and dizziness. After performing a routine examination, he asked her about her eating habits. Jill was extremely embarrassed and guilty about describing these to him, but she felt that the time had come to do something about her eating.

Jill confessed that she had a long-standing pattern of uncontrollably consuming extremely large quantities of food (known as binge eating) and then vomiting this food (purging). This binge-purge pattern began years ago, but it has become more severe and more frequent since she began working as a stewardess. Jill's doctor asked her to describe her eating pattern in more detail. Jill looked awkward and ashamed as she described her most recent binge: after getting home from a flight last night, she went out to a local market and bought a half-gallon of chocolate ice cream, a box of cookies, a medium-sized frozen pizza, a loaf of French bread, and a quart of milk. When she got home she ate everything she had bought as quickly as she could. Immediately afterward she ran to the bathroom, knelt in front of the toilet, thrust her fingers down her throat, and threw up everything she had just eaten.

According to Jill, this was a fairly typical amount of food for a binge, and she usually finishes eating it within thirty or forty minutes. She almost always induces vomiting right after binge eating, usually by sticking her fingers or occasionally other objects (e.g., a Popsicle stick or a spoon) down her throat. Jill admitted that her eating behavior was very strange, but she felt that she could not control it, especially when she was at home. Presently she goes through this binge-purge cycle once or twice a day when she is at home; she can control herself "on the road" and only rarely binges when she is traveling. On average, she estimates that she binges around eight times per week; she also takes "a handful" of laxatives once or twice a week after binge eating. (She estimates that she swallows about twelve to fifteen laxative pills at a time.) She also takes Lasix (a diuretic) and diet pills in an effort to lose weight.

It was very difficult for Jill to tell her doctor about her strange eating pattern, but she felt relieved once she had. Her doctor told her that she had a disorder called Bulimia Nervosa and referred her to an eating disorders clinic. Before her appointment at the clinic, Jill read several articles about this disorder and felt relieved to find out that other women suffered from these same uncontrollable symptoms. When her therapist asked her what brought her to the clinic, she merely looked down and replied, "I have bulimia."

In the course of her initial interview, Jill also admitted that she recently suffered from an episode of depression following a breakup with her boyfriend. During this depression she felt so despondent and weak that she occasionally missed work. Although she frequently had suicidal thoughts during this time and had even formulated several suicide plans, she did not make any actual suicide attempts. She reported that this episode lasted approximately a month and then seemed to lift by itself. She also reported a similar episode about two years earlier, following her withdrawal from college. She did not seek treatment for either of these episodes.

☐ PERSONAL HISTORY

Jill is the youngest of three daughters in what she considers to be a fairly average middle-class family. When asked if her parents had any psychological or medical problems, she described her father as having a minor alcohol problem and her mother as having occasional bouts of depression. Neither parent has ever been treated professionally. Jill reports that there was some degree of conflict between her parents, but she does not feel that they were unusual in this regard. According to her there is no history of abuse or neglect in her childhood.

Jill describes herself as having been preoccupied with her weight since she was 13. She was constantly concerned about being thin and making a good impression. At age 14 she reached her adult height of 5' 6' and weighed 130 pounds; she considered herself to be overweight. She dieted off and on for the next two years, but without any lasting success. When she was 16, a friend told her about self-induced vomiting. Although she was initially disgusted at the idea, she nevertheless tried this method one night after she had overeaten. She found that the vomiting was tolerable, and she quickly adopted this method as a clever trick to diet without being hungry. In her words, "Throwing up wasn't so bad; it sure beat trying so hard not to eat." During the next year she lost over 20 pounds. Over the next three years she used self-induced vomiting to maintain her weight.

When Jill was 17 she weighed 105 pounds and felt more or less satisfied with her weight. She decided to apply for a job as a model. The modeling agency did not hire her, saying that she should try to lose more weight. Discouraged, Jill gave up on modeling and, with the encouragement of her parents, enrolled in a local private university.

In college, Jill had more freedom to experiment with her eating habits. She discovered that by vomiting she could eat rather large amounts of food and still maintain her weight. Gradually her binge eating became more severe and more frequent, until she was eating huge amounts of food twice daily. It was now becoming more and more difficult to hide her odd eating behavior from her roommates, and on occasion she even stole food from them. Jill recalled one particularly embarrassing incident:

> Shelley had bought a bunch of ice cream and potato chips for a party for a club she was in. Well, I couldn't stand having all that stuff around, so I just went at it. Of course I had planned to replace it all, but I didn't get around to it before she got back. Boy, was she shocked to find all that stuff gone! I felt really bad and apologized . . . I made up a story about how some of my friends came over and we all couldn't resist it. She didn't say anything, but I think she knew what really happened.

At this time Jill also began abusing laxatives and diuretics. As her control over her eating weakened, she also began abusing alcohol. She said that she became intoxicated and vomited at almost every party she attended. By her junior year her binge eating and her alcohol abuse had begun to interfere with her social life and her academic performance. She began to feel weak and ill for long stretches, and she started missing assignments. She also began staying away from her friends on campus, partly because she felt so embarrassed and ashamed about her eating. During her junior year, Jill dropped out and worked as a receptionist. Relieved of the social pressures of campus life, she gradually decreased her binge eating to an average of twice a week over the next few years, and her weight increased to 135 pounds. Jill described being totally dissatisfied with herself at this time of her life. On the recommendation of a friend, she enrolled in a flight attendant training school.

Jill was surprised to find that the airline had a strict weight limit for their flight attendants. Trainees who were overweight were dropped from the program, and attendants who did not make their weight target were grounded. Worried that she would be cut from the program, Jill was now more weight conscious than ever before. She frantically sought ways to lose weight, and she began binge eating and purging two or three times daily. In addition she eliminated alcohol from her diet and ate only dietary foods (vegetables, diet soda, etc.) when she was not binge eating. After two months she had lost 20 pounds. She was now well within the airline's weight guidelines, and she also felt much better about her appearance. However, she had begun to feel weak and dizzy and was concerned that she was losing control over her eating. It was at this point that she consulted her doctor.

☐ CONCEPTUALIZATION AND TREATMENT

As Jill herself recognized, her frequent binge eating, her use of vomiting, laxatives, and diuretics as purging agents, and her constant concern with her weight were clear indications of Bulimia Nervosa. Most bulimics are fully aware of the unusual nature of their behavior; many even know the formal diagnostic label for their disorder. Nevertheless they report feeling unable to control their binge-purge cycles.

Jill's history contains many social and occupational pressures that induced her to focus on her appearance. Since puberty, maintaining a trim figure has been an important aspect of her life. Later, her social life at college and the strict weight requirements of her job as an airline attendant highlighted the importance of restricting her weight. For the past ten years bulimic eating has been an effective way for Jill to control her weight, and it seems reasonable to conclude that these factors may have contributed to her development of Bulimia Nervosa.

The initial focus of therapy was to alter Jill's bulimic eating pattern directly. After her evaluation interview, Jill was admitted as an outpatient in the eating disorders clinic. Jill's cognitive-behavioral therapy incorporated three general goals: (1) to identify the circumstances that surround her binge eating, (2) to restructure her thoughts about herself and her eating, and (3) to provide her with information on the risks of bulimic behavior, on meal planning and nutrition, and on the cultural standards that might intensify her bulimic behavior.

First, Jill was instructed to keep a detailed record of her actual eating behavior so that she and her therapist could examine the exact conditions associated with her binge eating. Jill was also told to note her moods in this record to see how her emotions were associated with her bulimic behavior. Jill's record showed that she frequently binged in the late afternoon and early evening, often after a particularly stressful therapy session or after returning from a long flight. The emotional entries in her record also showed that she felt a sense of relief following her binge-purge episodes. By analyzing this record, it was evident that Jill's bulimic behavior was often used as a way to cope with stressful events in her life.

Second, Jill's distorted and illogical self-cognitions regarding her body image and worth were addressed using a cognitive restructuring procedure. Through confrontive, Socratic dialogues in individual therapy, Jill was taught to review her thoughts and feelings, to identify her distorted or illogical thoughts, and to correct them. These cognitions might be brought up in therapy, or they might be taken from her record (or as Jill calls it, her "diary").

Jill: Well, here's one from my diary. When I tried on a pair of slacks, they were too tight. I felt really fat, and I was miserable for the rest of the day. I just felt worthless.

Therapist: Did you consider any other possibilities?

Jill: Like what?

Therapist: Maybe the slacks shrank in the laundry. Maybe it was humid and sticky, and they just felt tight. Or maybe they were just too small to begin with.

Jill: Sure, I guess it's possible, but I don't know. I mean, they fit before. I thought it meant that I was getting really fat.

Therapist: OK. Let's say that you really did gain a few pounds. So what?

Jill: So what!? It shows that I have to diet even harder because I'm getting obese!

Therapist: Let's look at some of your assumptions. It sounds to me like you have no middle ground; gaining a few pounds means being obese. Do you think that's really an indication of being obese?

Jill: No, I guess not.

Therapist: It also sounds to me like you have a lot of other assumptions about gaining weight. For instance, you feel that gaining a few pounds will make you a failure, and no one will love you or accept you if you do. Is that true?

Jill: Yeah. But the airline might ground me if I get too fat. I mean, it's a real worry.

Therapist: Then maybe being a flight attendant is not the right career for you.

Jill: But I like it. I don't want to quit.

Therapist: I'm not saying you have to. All I'm saying is that you should look at what it's doing to you and maybe consider other possibilities. OK?

Jill: OK.

In addition to her individual therapy, Jill also attended group therapy sessions. Mostly these group sessions focused on sharing experiences with other bulimics and fostering a sense of mutual support. In particular, the group members discussed the difficulty they had in controlling their binge eating, and they offered to be available if any member of the group needed support or encouragement.

The third goal of therapy was to provide Jill with information regarding various aspects of her eating disorder. First, the emotional and physical risks inherent in the binge-purge cycle (social isolation, salt and water imbalances, gastrointestinal irritations, tooth decay through the erosion of tooth enamel, etc.) were described. Second, Jill was taught to plan reasonable meals for herself. She was given homework assignments that required her to research the nutritional value of various foods and to formulate healthy meal plans. Most important, she was to eat these meals. Third, Jill was taught to recognize our culture's expectations and norms regarding appearances and weight. In Jill's case, the norms of her airline were clear and explicit. For most bulimics, however, the expectations of our society (often conveyed through the entertainment and advertising industries) are more subtle and more difficult to identify.

Jill was treated for a total of twenty weeks. For the first two weeks her meals were planned for her. She found it difficult to follow these plans without binge eating now and then. During this time she reported vomiting eight times after meals. Still, Jill was making progress over her pretreatment rate. For the next several weeks Jill devised her own meal plans with the help of the staff. She found that having planned her own meals made it a little easier to stick to the diet. Gradually she reduced the frequency of her vomiting until she had stopped completely by the seventeenth week. After three weeks of relatively normal eating behavior, Jill discontinued treatment. She was encouraged to follow her meal plans and to contact her therapist or a therapy group member if she felt that she was having trouble controlling her eating behavior.

◻ PROGNOSIS

Jill's treatment appears to have been effective in altering her bulimic eating patterns. In a letter she wrote to her therapist approximately two months after she ended therapy, Jill stated that she has binged and vomited only twice since her last session. She reported eating more healthy and balanced meals (both at home and during her layovers) and feeling more energetic and active. Jill also said that she feels better about herself and her appearance, and she does not feel as "stressed" after difficult flights as she used to. In short, therapy seems to have greatly reduced the frequency of Jill's binging and purging, and it seems to have created enhanced feelings of self-worth that may help prevent these symptoms from reappearing in the future.

Despite Jill's obvious improvement, however, her prognosis must remain guarded. Bulimia Nervosa is a persistent eating disorder, and it has proven very difficult to effect lasting behavioral changes in those who suffer from it. Research on treatment for bulimics has begun only recently, and the limited information that is available is not optimistic. About half of the bulimics who improved in therapy relapsed within eighteen months. Thus while Jill's therapy seems to be successful for the present, it is quite possible that she might resume her binge eating and purging patterns, perhaps as a reaction to some future stressful life event.

◻ DISCUSSION

The specific causes of Bulimia Nervosa are not yet known, and there are great variations from case to case in the presenting complaints and personal histories. However, it is generally agreed that bulimics put an inordinate amount of importance on their physical appearance in determining their self-esteem, and this preoccupation probably contributes to their development of the disorder. For most bulimics, these cognitions usually have been evident for years. In addition, there is some evidence that certain cultural or occupational demands (or both) may exacerbate this behavior. For example, researchers have found a higher prevalence of Bulimia Nervosa (and Anorexia Nervosa, see below) in people with careers that involve strict standards for physical appearance (e.g., dancing, acting, modeling, athletics, etc.). While these external expectations may not have caused bulimics to develop their odd eating patterns, they do appear to be a factor in maintaining the disorder.

In a discussion of Bulimia Nervosa, it is important to distinguish this disorder from Anorexia Nervosa, another serious eating disorder. In fact, these two disorders do share many common features. Their victims are primarily young females who are overly concerned with maintaining a slim figure and have a rather distorted view of their own body image. In addition, these two disorders often overlap; approximately half of the anorexics have engaged in some form of bulimic behavior, and many bulimics have a history of significant caloric restriction. Despite these similarities, Bulimia Nervosa and Anorexia Nervosa are disorders with distinct features. Anorexia Nervosa is characterized by maintenance of a dangerously low body weight (at least 15% below the minimum normal weight), usually by a severe restriction of food intake that seems to involve a startling degree of self-control. Anorexics are consequently jeopardized by severe medical complications including malnutrition, metabolic changes, and amenorrhea (a cessation of menstrual discharge). Most anorexics deny their disorder and are unwilling to receive treatment for it. In contrast, most bulimics are of approximately normal weight and are only rarely in any serious medical danger. The primary concern for bulimics involves the social complications that arise from these patterns. Their attempts to hide their disorder and their feelings of guilt and shame about their binges and purges lead many bulimics to isolate themselves from friends and family members. In addition, many bulimics suffer from the physical side effects of their purging: gastrointestinal difficulties, eroded tooth enamel, electrolyte imbalances, and the like. The majority of bulimics recognize that their eating behavior is abnormal. Due to recent coverage of Bulimia Nervosa in the popular media, many bulimics are quite sophisticated about the nature of their disorder. Nevertheless, most bulimics are unable to control their binge eating and purging.

The DSM-III-R criteria for Bulimia Nervosa specify that someone with this disorder must have had an average of at least two binge-eating episodes per week for at least three months. (These criteria are considered useful to distinguish true bulimics from the common college student who overeats occasionally.) Actually the "casual binger" rarely seeks therapy; the majority of bulimics who are treated have a five- to fifteen-year history of clear binge eating and purging.

The binges described by Jill are typical of most bulimics. Binge foods are usually high-caloric foods rich in complex carbohydrates (sugars and starches) and fat. Typically these foods are eaten very quickly. Binges are usually followed almost immediately by purging, usually self-induced vomiting. In fact, the goal of most binges seems to be the inducement of the following purge. It appears that the goal of a binge may be the distended feeling that leads to the purge, not the enjoyment of the binge food itself.

The psychological reactions that Jill had to her eating behavior are also typical. Many bulimics feel guilt and shame over their uncontrolled eating behavior. Others report a feeling of "psychological numbing" or relief following the binge-purge cycle. This relief does not seem to be specific to any particular mood; bulimics have reported that their binges reduce their level of anxiety, depression, anger, and even elation. Thus it seems that for some bulimics, their binge eating serves as a buffer that insulates them from stressful (and even pleasurable) emotional states.

There are also indications of a possible association between Bulimia Nervosa and feelings of depression. Depression is often noted as part of a bulimic's presenting complaint. In addition, the medical and psychiatric histories of bulimics and their families often reveal a high incidence of mood disorders (usually Dysthymic Disorder or Major Depression, see Case 6). Furthermore, antidepressants have proven to be more effective than placebos in the treatment of Bulimia Nervosa. Thus it is important to assess a bulimic's level of depression at the initiation of treatment. Presently, about one-fourth of the bulimics who receive therapy are prescribed antidepressants, primarily tricyclics.

As in Jill's case, cognitive-behavioral therapy for Bulimia Nervosa is relatively brief, lasting anywhere from two to six months. Although it is not common for therapy to last more than six months, some programs last much longer. Since the primary goal of treatment is to regularize the patients' eating patterns, some treatment programs routinely hospitalize bulimics in order to monitor and control their eating behavior more closely. Most programs, however, begin treatment on an outpatient basis. When these patients end therapy, they are encouraged to follow a regular eating routine that includes healthy, nutritious food and a strict avoidance of any dieting. Bulimics have been found to be more susceptible to relapse if they deviate from a regularized eating schedule. Follow-up studies indicate that approximately 60 percent of the bulimics treated with cognitive-behavioral therapy show some improvement, and about half of these patients maintain these therapy gains for at least eighteen months. Traditional psychodynamic therapy has also been utilized with this population, but with less success. However, many behavior therapists concede that bulimics with particularly chronic or persistent symptoms, especially those who are also depressed, may derive some benefit from traditional, long-term psychotherapy.

AUTISTIC DISORDER

Behavior Modification

☐ **PRESENTING COMPLAINT**

Tommy is a cute, 5-year-old boy with straight brown hair and bright blue eyes. Except for his slightly crooked teeth and a somewhat blank expression on his face, he looks just like any other boy his age. After watching Tommy for just a short time, however, it becomes readily apparent that he suffers from severe abnormalities that seem to affect virtually every aspect of his life: his speech, his thinking, his actions, and his relationships with others.

The first obvious sign of Tommy's psychological impairment is his speech. Except for occasional unintelligible grunts, Tommy is virtually mute. In the first five years of his life he has learned only a few signed words using American Sign Language (ASL). He can gesture for "more," "eat," and "toilet" (by signing "T"). He also tries to communicate by pointing at people, places, and objects, but most often the intent of these nonspecific gestures is not clear. Other than these rudimentary sounds and gestures, Tommy has no real linguistic ability.

Tommy's IQ, as measured on the Wechsler Intelligence Scale for Children-Revised (WISC-R) is 48, which would categorize him as moderately retarded. However, because of his pervasive lack of communication skills and his lack of interest in testing procedures, it is difficult to assess accurately the extent of his cognitive impairment.

What is easier to assess is Tommy's odd behavior. Frequently Tommy will sit with his arms grasping his chest or his knees and slowly rock back and forth, all the while staring straight ahead. Tommy also engages in other forms of repetitive behavior, such as pushing a toy car back and forth (often not on its wheels) and drawing page after page of parallel straight lines. It is not uncommon for these seemingly meaningless behaviors to last for four or five hours without interruption. At these times Tommy shows little emotion and seems totally engrossed in his ritualistic behavior. In the past few months, Tommy's hand has become the center of focus for many of his strange behaviors. He will suddenly stop what he is doing, hold his little hand directly in front of his face, and stare intently at it, usually rotating it slowly. As he examines his hand, he sometimes emits a high-pitched squealing tone; occasionally he smiles and giggles. Usually, though, he simply stares at it. He seems to be especially interested if his hand is covered with food (which is often the case at mealtimes) or is wet and dripping.

In addition to these strange, repetitive behaviors, Tommy also has bursts of wild, uncontrolled activity, usually when he is upset. Sometimes he will run around with his legs pumping and his arms flailing, screaming the whole time. At other times he will pound his fists against the floor or a wall in an angry, frustrated tantrum. Often when he is examining his hand he will suddenly begin to shake it so violently that it appears as if he were trying to separate his hand from his arm. This sort of flailing is termed "hand flapping." On rare occasions Tommy manages to bite his hand while flapping, usually hard enough to break the skin. In the midst of these wild behaviors Tommy appears to be genuinely upset; his face grows red and his whole body seems tense. When he is restrained during these uncontrolled actions, he usually struggles for a few moments and then inexplicably goes about his business as if nothing had happened, seemingly as oblivious of the person who stopped him as he is of the actions themselves.

Another important aspect of Tommy's disorder, especially to his family, is his complete inability (or unwillingness) to form interpersonal relationships. During his short life Tommy has never engaged in any meaningful communication with others, not even at the level of establishing sustained direct eye contact. He seems to understand that people exist, and he even reacts to them occasionally; however, he does not seem to attach any special significance to other people as fellow human beings. For the most part he treats other people as mere objects—to be noticed, ignored, or avoided, much like most people treat large animals or pieces of furniture. Tommy does appear to attach some special significance to his parents; he will look at them when they address him and will pay attention to their actions. Even this relationship is very distant, though. Maybe the best description for his relationship with his parents is that he treats them like two strangers on a busy city street: He seems to understand that they are fellow humans and may even be temporarily interested in what they are doing, but he seems to have no particular interest in establishing any sort of meaningful relationship with them.

For the first two years of his life, Tommy was an unusually quiet and independent child. Strangely, he would ignore his parents, his brother, and relatives who came to visit. His parents believed that his odd behavior was something that he would eventually outgrow; but after Tommy turned 3, it became obvious that he was seriously impaired. They took him to a number of pediatricians, who diagnosed him as suffering from a pervasive developmental disorder commonly referred to as childhood autism. At first Tommy's parents attempted to take care of him at home. After a few months, however, they brought him to a special school for autistic children.

☐ PERSONAL HISTORY

Tommy is the younger child of two in an upper-middle-class family living in a prestigious suburb north of Milwaukee. Tommy's father is a senior vice president of a medium-sized manufacturing firm, and his mother is an associate professor at a large state university in Milwaukee. Tommy's brother, who is four years older, is successful in school and popular with his friends.

His mother described Tommy during his infancy as a "model baby." He was always quiet and hardly ever cried or fussed. However, from early on it was difficult for Tommy's parents to get his attention or make eye contact. He was unresponsive to games such as "peek-a-boo," and he did not demonstrate any need to be held or comforted. As noted earlier, although his parents thought these traits were somewhat peculiar, they did not worry about them at first.

When he was 2½ years old, Tommy was enrolled in day care. Initially Tommy was considered a quiet, cooperative child, but gradually his inability to interact with other people in a meaningful way was becoming more noticeable. At day care, Tommy spent most his day silently staring off into the distance or rocking by himself in a corner. Over the next six months Tommy increased the frequency of his odd repetitive behaviors and also began to throw tantrums and run around wildly. Since these behaviors began to disrupt the day-care routine, Tommy's parents were asked to remove him. They hired a private sitter to stay with him during the day; but after eight months three sitters had already quit, and it was becoming clear that he required special care.

By this time Tommy had still not begun to talk, and his parents began to worry seriously about his intellectual abilities. He was taken to numerous pediatric and neurology specialists, who said that Tommy suffered from an autistic disorder and would need to be institutionalized. Realizing his need for special care but reluctant to institutionalize him, Tommy's parents hired a private pediatric nurse to stay with him. Over the next year, Tommy's disruptive tantrums and running around became more frequent and more severe. In addition, Tommy began to flap and bite his hand. His parents and the nurse had to monitor his behavior constantly to make sure he did not cause costly damage to the house or serious injury to himself. After about a year the private nurse quit, and Tommy's mother was forced to take a semester leave to look after him. Finally she contacted a day school for autistic and emotionally disturbed children. ("Emotionally disturbed" is a global term that describes a range of problems, including severe shyness and withdrawal and disabling anxiety.) After being on the waiting list for approximately four months, a space opened up, and Tommy was enrolled.

☐ CONCEPTUALIZATION AND TREATMENT

Like the specialists Tommy had been taken to earlier, the staff at the special school had no difficulty diagnosing him as having Autistic Disorder. Autistic Disorder, commonly referred to as childhood autism, is a pervasive developmental disorder that affects almost every aspect of the child's life. The primary feature of autism, which literally means "self-ism," is the child's inability to form meaningful relationships with other people and a more or less complete withdrawal into a private world. This profound social withdrawal is usually accompanied by severe disturbances in the child's intellectual and linguistic abilities; most autistic children are mentally retarded and have very limited, if any, communication skills. In addition, autistic children are characterized by odd behaviors, typically consisting of meaningless repetitious behaviors and bursts of wild activity. Many autistic children also engage in any of a variety of self-mutilating behaviors, including hand biting, scratching and gouging, head banging, and pica (eating nonnutritive substances such as paste or feces).

Tommy clearly fits this mold. Throughout his short life he has been unable to form an adequate relationship with anyone—including the other children at his day-care center, his sitters, or even his parents. His intellectual skills are severely impaired, and his communication skills are virtually nonexistent. His meaningless rocking, playing, and drawing, his wild flapping, and his frequent tantrums all provide additional behavioral evidence of his Autistic Disorder.

Tommy was enrolled in the school for autistic and emotionally disturbed children in November. During the academic year, the school runs from 8:30 A.M. to 4:30 P.M. on weekdays. The staff consists of nonmedical personnel with doctorates or master's degrees in Clinical Psychology and Special Education. There are five full-time therapists, one occupational therapist, and two speech therapists, and several volunteers from local colleges and high schools. The pupils range in age from 5 to 25 years and are drawn from the entire Milwaukee metropolitan area. The number of pupils varies; with eighteen, the school is presently filled to capacity. Fourteen of the children are autistic like Tommy. (Tommy is one of the most severely disturbed children in the school.) Four are diagnosed as emotionally disturbed (ED). As with autistic children, the extreme shyness, withdrawal, and anxiety of ED children seriously impair their social development. These children are so intimidated by interpersonal situations that their scholastic performance also suffers. However, emotionally disturbed children differ from autistic children in that they are able to perceive their social environment relatively well, and as a rule they do not exhibit the uncontrolled and bizarre symptoms of the autistic children.

Tommy's school also runs an eight-week live-in summer camp, where the students are supervised twenty-four hours a day. The staff at the camp consists of one staff member from the school, who acts as a supervisor, and six trained undergraduate counselors. The number of students who may attend the camp at any one time is limited to seven. Since there is a long waiting list, the younger and more disturbed children are limited to two weeks at the camp. The older and more capable students are allowed to stay the entire eight weeks. Being the youngest and one of the most severely disturbed children in the school, Tommy was limited to a two-week stay during his first two summers.

Tommy's school employs a behavioral model of treatment. The primary focus of the staff is not to "cure" the students but to teach them some basic skills that may help them lead more independent lives. The therapists attempt to achieve this goal by carefully controlling the children's environment, particularly the level of reinforcement (and occasionally punishment) the children receive. The more formal classroom instruction (conducted both in groups and on a one-to-one basis) concentrates on providing the children with opportunities to develop social and cognitive skills. Social interaction and basic hygiene are taught through less formal instruction, which is conducted just about anywhere: on the playground, in the cafeteria, and even in the bathrooms. Since therapy relies to such a great extent on controlling the children's social environments, parents are encouraged to adopt behavioral techniques at home to help maintain the gains made at school.

Group lessons take several forms; their general aim is to teach the students to cooperate with one another. For example, in a shared finger-painting task, each child starts a picture and then exchanges pictures with another student. The children are reinforced for allowing another student to work on "their" project, and they are given special rewards for working on a project together. In another group activity, this time conducted at the swing set on the playground, students are assigned either to ride on a swing or to push another student. Again, the children are reinforced for displaying cooperation and reciprocity. During these sessions the therapists have to be careful to notice whenever a student behaves appropriately and to reinforce that student as soon as possible through encouragement, hugs, and occasionally snacks.

Individual therapy focuses on developing the children's cognitive and linguistic skills. For example, the therapist might employ flash cards and practice booklets to work on a student's vocabulary or basic math skills. In addition, each child meets with a speech therapist for fifty minutes every other day to practice his or her diction or, in the case of more severely disturbed children, their signing. Every student is also instructed in basic vocational skills (e.g., matching wires by colors, sorting various nuts and bolts, sweeping the work area, etc.). This training is considered especially important because a job in a sheltered workshop is probably the only employment opportunity most of these children will ever have.

In addition to these relatively formal lessons, the staff takes every opportunity to teach the students basic life skills. During lunch the staff attempts to monitor closely the students' behavior, and students are reinforced for such things as waiting in line cooperatively, eating with others, not playing with their food, chewing their food sufficiently, and not causing disturbances (throwing their food, taking other students' food, running or screaming, etc.). Similar practical training takes place in the bathrooms. Although every student is already toilet trained (it is a requirement for admission to the school), accidents are not uncommon among the younger and more disturbed children. The students have to be carefully monitored to ensure that they perform the common steps of toileting that most people take for granted (i.e., putting the toilet seat up/down; making sure to urinate/defecate *in* the toilet, not on or around it; wiping themselves adequately; flushing the toilet; washing afterward; etc.). The staff considers teaching the students these basic life skills to be a vital step in helping them develop a greater degree of independence.

Developing these basic life skills is the primary focus of the summer camp. Students (called "campers") are taught to perform a variety of everyday tasks such as cleaning their room, doing their laundry, taking a shower, and preparing for bed. Each of these basic tasks is broken up into smaller, more manageable subtasks. For example, getting the campers ready for bed involves several individual components: having them pick up their toys and clothes, changing into their pajamas, brushing their teeth, and so on. The other focus of the summer camp is to develop the campers' social skills. This training occurs primarily during recreational activities and at mealtimes.

The school uses a variety of reinforcers to reward appropriate behavior. Most important, secondary reinforcement in the form of attention, praise, encouragement, and hugs is given to every student. However, since one of the primary characteristics of autistic children is a marked disinterest in interpersonal relationships, this social reinforcement is usually supplemented by more tangible rewards, such as candy and snacks. As the students become used to the structure of the program, their privileges (e.g., recess time, dessert at lunch, etc.) become used as reinforcements with increasing frequency. This is especially true at the summer camp, where the students' recreational activities (swimming, hiking, playing, etc.), their participation on field trips, and even the opportunity to choose preferred foods are contingent on their behavior.

Eliminating inappropriate behavior is more difficult. In many cases it is assumed that secondary reinforcers—such as the staff's attention and concern—work to maintain inappropriate actions. The staff attempts to extinguish these actions by withdrawing positive reinforcement, that is, by ignoring them. Since negative behavior can be very disrupting to the other students, especially during group lessons, often these behaviors are extinguished by placing the child in a separate room commonly referred to as a "time-out room." Occasionally the children are punished by scolding them or withdrawing their privileges.

Sometimes a child exhibits odd behavior that demands close supervision. For example, one autistic girl had a persistent habit involving pica. She would hide in a bathroom stall until no one was around, defecate, and quickly eat her own feces. When the therapists noticed that she was not with the other students, they would run to the bathroom and most often catch her in the act. Her habit took on the air of an addiction: when she had eaten her own feces she appeared to be content, although the act seemed rushed and forced; when she was interrupted and prevented from eating her feces, she became very upset. The staff was careful to prevent this behavior and reinforce her for flushing her feces. They also (sometimes in spite of themselves) scolded her for this behavior. Over the course of four months, her pica was gradually eliminated, presumably as a result of the staff's efforts.

For the first few days of school, Tommy was extremely upset. He threw frequent tantrums (around four or five per day) and spent most of his time flapping his hand or rocking quietly in a corner. Soon he became accustomed to the school routine, though, and it became possible to engage him in the daily lessons. By the holiday break in December, Tommy had grown to expect the daily routine of the school and in fact became very distressed when it was interrupted by the vacation.

To enable Tommy to benefit from the school setting, the staff initially concentrated on eliminating his disruptive behaviors. When he threw a tantrum, the staff was careful to ignore him. If the tantrum persisted, or if it was interrupting a group lesson, Tommy was placed in the time-out room for ten minutes or until his tantrum ended. During the next few weeks Tommy's tantrums became less and less frequent, and by the first vacation break they had virtually ceased. Tommy's parents, who were also instructed to use this extinction procedure, reported that he had stopped throwing tantrums at home as well.

The staff employed a shaping technique to control Tommy's hand flapping and wild running around. When these actions began he would be physically restrained by a staff member. Usually he would resist this restraint by squirming or shouting. If he started to calm down, however, he was given a reward. Effective reinforcements for him were M&Ms, peanuts, and apple juice. After several incidents Tommy learned to calm down merely in response to the staff's commands and requests. Now he was reinforced for stopping his disruptive behavior only if he did not need to be restrained. Later, as Tommy learned to remain quiet after calming down, his reinforcement became contingent on remaining in control for a set period of time, first ten minutes, then fifteen, then thirty, and so on. After six months, Tommy's hand flapping and uncontrolled running was reduced to its present level. Although he still performs these disruptive actions on occasion, he does so much less frequently than he used to, and he usually stops this behavior after a short warning from a staff member.

The next focus of therapy was to increase Tommy's level of social interaction. When Tommy arrived at the school, he made no effort to communicate with the staff or his fellow students. In fact, he gave no sign of recognizing them other than as inanimate objects. By selectively reinforcing his cooperative play and recreation behaviors, the staff gradually got Tommy to participate in group recreation projects and unstructured play activities. However, the changes have been very slow and gradual, and even after two years Tommy still gives little indication that he regards people with any level of empathy or interpersonal understanding.

The overriding goal of Tommy's more formal lessons and his speech therapy was to increase his vocabulary. After more than two years of intensive individual and group therapy, Tommy's vocabulary has increased from 3 words to slightly over 100. Throughout the first year, Tommy refused to make any attempt at verbal communication. As a result, most of his speech training consisted of teaching him the ASL sign for various objects and concepts in his world (e.g., "teacher," "hungry," "outside," etc.). During the training sessions, Tommy was rewarded for making various signs demonstrated by the speech therapist or shown on cue cards. During his second year, Tommy began to verbalize the words he was learning. As was the case with his other training, Tommy was selectively reinforced for making closer and closer approximations to the words' actual sounds. Although his articulation is very poor and the majority of his speech is incomprehensible to most people, his willingness to verbalize some of this thoughts represents a great advancement in his communication skills.

During summer camp Tommy's training concentrated on more basic life skills, particularly his eating behavior and his personal hygiene. When Tommy arrived at camp, he did not use eating utensils. Furthermore, he was an unusually impatient and sloppy eater; his place at the cafeteria table was always marked by a large amount of spilled food. Occasionally he would throw relatively large food items (pieces of bread, sausage links, etc.) around the cafeteria, often hitting other campers or staff members. Since most of his lunches at school consisted of sandwiches and treats, the extent to which he lacked proper eating skills was not readily apparent until his arrival at camp. By using his dessert or favorite foods as rewards, Tommy was taught to eat with utensils and to keep most of his food on his tray. After two weeks of careful monitoring by the staff, Tommy by and large had stopped throwing food and had begun to use a fork sporadically. Unfortunately, his eating habits were not otherwise affected by his camp experiences.

Another aspect of Tommy's disorder that was not fully appreciated until he arrived at camp was his need to have order, predictability, and routine in his everyday life. For example, part of Tommy's training took place in the shower, where he was taught to wash himself thoroughly. It soon became clear that Tommy had a set ritual when he washed himself: left foot first, then left leg, then left side, then left arm, and so on. If he performed this washing ritual out of sequence or forgot a step, he would become very upset and would insist on repeating the entire ritual again. It was not uncommon for Tommy to spend over two hours in the shower, with the counselor standing with him in the shower the entire time. In an attempt to get Tommy to give up this ritual, the counselors scheduled his showers directly before his most preferred activities, swimming and hiking. Although his showers became somewhat shorter, his shower ritual did not change significantly. On several occasions he forsook his favorite activities because of this ritual. Tommy's second stay as a camper similarly had little effect on his shower ritual. Apparently it was more important for Tommy to complete his ritualistic behavior than to participate in his favorite recreation events.

☐ PROGNOSIS

After over two years at the school (including two camp sessions), Tommy has made some limited improvement. His vocabulary has increased to over 100 words, and he is beginning to develop his speech skills. Tommy is also capable of performing some simple addition problems. For the most part, though, the progress in his communication and academic skills has been very slow, and his IQ has not changed significantly. The most noticeable change appears to be a reduction in Tommy's disruptive behaviors. His temper tantrums have for the most part stopped, and the amount of time he spends flapping his hand and running around wildly has been greatly reduced. In short, he is generally calmer in most situations and much easier to control. In addition, Tommy is more able to cooperate with others during games and when working on recreation projects. Still, the staff and Tommy's parents get the impression that his cooperation is merely in response to their expectations; he doesn't seem to be particularly interested in forming relationships with others. He still spends most of his free time absently playing with his favorite toys, staring at his hand, or just rocking quietly.

As has been the case with Tommy, therapy with most autistic children is a slow and frustrating process. Although gradual improvements are generally achieved through behavioral regimes, noteworthy changes are rare. Because the children's home environments are usually less stringently controlled than their therapeutic ones, setbacks are frequent, especially after weekends and vacation breaks. It is also difficult for therapists to maintain the level of observation and control necessary for the behavioral program.

In general, the prognosis for children with Autistic Disorder is poor. Some of the less disturbed children may eventually be able to live relatively independently in a supervised apartment or halfway house and may hold down a steady job in a sheltered work environment. A child's early speech skills generally serve as a good, although rough, indicator of his or her prognosis. By and large, children who have developed recognizable speech by the age of 5 will be able to benefit most from therapy and perhaps eventually live on their own. Most of the more severely disturbed children, however, will probably need to be institutionalized for the rest of their lives.

☐ DISCUSSION

Tommy's case is typical of a child with a severe Autistic Disorder. Social withdrawal and self-absorption, poor speech and communication skills, retarded academic achievement, apparently meaningless disruptive behaviors, and a strong need to maintain a ritualized or routinized personal world are characteristics that are common to all children with this baffling disorder. Although Tommy's case history is representative of this disorder, there are several noteworthy characteristics of autism that were not evident in this case description.

First, Tommy's case represents a child who is severely autistic. Children who are less profoundly disturbed are able to attain much higher levels of academic achievement and communication skills. According to their IQ scores, approximately one-fourth of autistic children are not mentally retarded; these children often demonstrate bizarre, disruptive behavior only when they are under stress (e.g., being scolded or having their daily routine disrupted). Virtually all autistic children, however, suffer from significantly impaired social relationships, ranging from chronic feelings of loneliness to an utter inability to form meaningful interpersonal relationships.

Second, isolated but widely publicized cases have reported autistic children who possess some extraordinarily well-developed ability, usually in the area of mathematical calculation or the manipulation of spatial forms. For example, Daniel, a 16-year-old student at Tommy's school, could mentally add, subtract, multiply, and even divide ten-digit numbers. He also knew virtually every statistic available for every player who was ever a member of the Green Bay Packers (round drafted into the pros; number of tackles; rushing, receiving, and passing yardage; etc.) In another case, a 5-year-old autistic girl was able to draw beautiful sketches of horses, roosters, and other animals with uncanny sophistication. Unfortunately, the abilities of these *idiot-savants*, or "wise idiots," is usually limited to a narrow range of talents that are almost never of any practical use. In fact, their extreme level of focus and the uniqueness of their abilities seem to have the effect of emphasizing the differences between them and most other children. Thus their unusual abilities may actually exacerbate the social isolation so characteristic of this disorder.

A third point to note is that initially most psychodynamic theorists attributed the development of this disorder to the child's reaction to cold, unfeeling parents. These parents, often called "emotional refrigerators," were typically very successful professionals who were seen as either too intellectual or too busy to establish an adequate emotional relationship with their infants. On the surface Tommy's parents, both successful professionals, seem to fit this pattern.

However, many experts have questioned this "emotional refrigerator" hypothesis. First, there has been little evidence that highly intelligent or successful parents interact with their children any differently than other parents. Second, apart from rare exceptions, the siblings of autistic children show no evidence of the disorder, so it seems unlikely that the actions of the parents per se are solely, or even partly, at fault for their children's disorder. Third, recent studies have provided some evidence that autism is a result of genetic or biochemical causes (or both), not psychogenic factors. Thus it seems plausible that the diagnosis of autistic disorder was more prevalent in the children of educated and successful parents simply because these children were more likely to be taken to specialists and enrolled in special programs, and were therefore more likely to receive this diagnosis. Despite these criticisms, psychogenic theories of childhood autism are still popular. Unfortunately, the primary impact of these theories seems to be on the parents of autistic children, whose hardships and frustrations are compounded by heightened feelings of guilt and failure. In contrast, biomedical and behavioral approaches to childhood autism relieve parents of the responsibility for their children's misfortunes, and the utility of these approaches may lie as much in helping to alleviate the guilt and despair of these parents as in teaching skills to the autistic children themselves.

Finally, it is important to note that the behaviors of autistic children —both their wild and disruptive actions and their persistent rejection of social attachments—are very taxing for the people who must deal with them on a regular basis, mostly their parents and the therapeutic staff. At Tommy's school the staff often joked that the eight-hour school days—and especially the eight-week summer camp—were more therapeutic for the parents of the students than for the students themselves. There seems to be some validity to this comment. Many staff members lost motivation in the face of the slow progress of their students. During Tommy's first two years at the school, for example, two full-time staff members quit and had to be replaced, and there was constant turnover in the student volunteer program. The summer camp counselors were especially prone to burnout. Although none of the camp counselors (all Psychology and Special Education majors) quit during either summer camp session, none returned for a second year, and only one of the twelve decided to pursue a career in mental health. In short, although some recent studies seem to be making progress in determining the cause of childhood autism, therapy for these children remains, at best, a difficult and frustrating process.